The Wolves of
World War II

The Wolves of World War II

An East Prussian Soldier's Memoir of Combat and Captivity on the Eastern Front

HANS THIEL

Translated and edited by Ivan Fehrenbach

Foreword by John K. Roth

McFarland & Company, Inc., Publishers
Jefferson, North Carolina, and London

LIBRARY OF CONGRESS CATALOGUING-IN-PUBLICATION DATA

Thiel, Hans, 1902–1974.
 The wolves of World War II: an East Prussian soldier's memoir
of combat and captivity on the Eastern Front / Hans Thiel ;
translated and edited by Ivan Fehrenbach ; foreword by John K.
Roth.
  p.   cm.
 Includes bibliographical references and index.

 ISBN-13: 978-0-7864-2971-4
 (softcover : 50# alkaline paper) ∞

 1. Thiel, Hans, 1902–1974. 2. Thiel, Hans, 1902–1974 —
Imprisonment. 3. World War, 1939–1945 — Germany — Biography.
4. World War, 1939–1945 — Campaigns — Eastern Front. 5. World
War, 1939–1945 — Personal narratives, German. 6. Soldiers —
Germany — Biography. 7. Prisoners of war — Germany — Biography.
8. Prisoners of war — Russia — Biography. 9. Prisoners of war —
Poland — Biography. 10. Germany — Politics and government — 1933–
1945. 11. Totalitarianism. I. Fehrenbach, Ivan, 1978– II. Title.
D757.3.T485A3   2007
940.54'7247092 — dc22   [B]   2006102716

British Library cataloguing data are available

On the cover: Wolves ©2007 Design Pics; fire and barbwire ©2007
PhotoSpin; hammer and sickle, Polish heraldic shield and swastika
vexilla-mundi.com

Manufactured in the United States of America

McFarland & Company, Inc., Publishers
 Box 611, Jefferson, North Carolina 28640
  www.mcfarlandpub.com

To Captain Gus,
an old German and great father

Acknowledgments

The research required to bring Hans Thiel's manuscript to its current state was truly a collaborative effort, and a number of people should be thanked for their assistance in the project. I am grateful to Ronald Bachman in the Library of Congress; to Peter Dembowski and Katarzyna Litynska for answering questions about the Polish and Russian languages; to David B. Morris in the Library of Congress; to Carol Poore, Elsa Diduk, and Hanni Sherman for answering questions about the German language and German-related issues; to Cynthia Smith in the Library of Congress for her assistance with the maps; to Dr. Robert Hardi for answering medical questions; and also to Alan Burke, Andy Franck, Trotter Hardy, Katie Hayes, John K. Roth, Martin E. Silfen, Peter Van Bergen, Arnold Weinstein, and the staff in general at the Library of Congress. My thanks to all of these people for their special expertise in a variety of subjects.

I would also like to thank the Thiel family (especially Dr. Martin Thiel and Anne Kane Thiel) for providing all of the personal information about Hans Thiel and his family. Thanks to Paul Thiel and Molly Thiel as well, and to Matthew Thiel for answering my many other questions and bringing me his great-uncle's manuscript in the first place.

In addition, I must express my deep gratitude to my family and other friends for their support — and I am particularly grateful to my father, whose help, encouragement, and friendship was a welcome combination, especially given the complexity and gravity of some of the subject matter.

Dr. Martin Thiel provides the dedication to a person I never met but to whom I am nevertheless greatly indebted: August Thiel, the brother of Hans Thiel, to whom the memoirist sent the manuscript and who then preserved it for over fifty years for later generations to read.

That leads me to the person who deserves the most credit in this book: Hans Thiel himself. If working with the events of this manuscript was at times difficult and troubling — as indeed it often was — I can only imagine living with the experiences. We must all thank Hans Thiel for having the courage to relive those experiences in his writing.

— Ivan Fehrenbach

Table of Contents

Foreword

by John K. Roth

On February 18, 1943, with the tides of war already turned decisively against the Third Reich, Joseph Goebbels, the German propaganda minister under Adolf Hitler, spurred his nation to "total war." Nazi Germany fought on for more than two years, but when unconditional surrender came in early May 1945, the German cost for Nazism had become incalculable.

Much of the price was paid by German villages and farms and by the men, women and children, including Hans Thiel (1902–74) and his family, who inhabited them. The penalty also fell heavily on large German cities and their populations. Hamburg was one of the striking examples. During July 1943, Allied bombers aimed to obliterate it. In his book *On the Natural History of Destruction*, the German novelist and essayist W. G. Sebald (1944–2001) states that one raid during the early morning of July 27 unloaded "ten thousand tons of high-explosive and incendiary bombs" on Hamburg, engulfing a densely populated district in "a firestorm of an intensity that no one would ever before have thought possible."[1]

Sebald's judgment came more than fifty years after that destructive summer morning. It was informed by the insight of another German novelist and essayist, Hans Erich Nossack (1901–77), who saw Hamburg's destruction firsthand. Three months later, he wrote a memoir about what he had witnessed. Like Hans Thiel's *The Wolves of World War II*, Nossack's account was not translated into English until the twenty-first century. The German title of Nossack's narrative, however, will be familiar to moviegoers who have seen Oliver Hirschbiegel's

1

significant 2004 film about the last days of Hitler in April 1945, when the Red Army, encountered earlier by Thiel farther east, stormed Berlin and dealt final crushing blows to the Nazi regime. The English-language version rendered *Der Untergang*, the film's German title, as *The Downfall*, but when Joel Agee translated Nossack's description of Hamburg's destruction, which had that same German title, he called it *The End*. Both concepts —*downfall* and *end*— aptly identify what Nossack experienced, and they also have their place as one reads Thiel's testament, which has been so well translated and contextualized by Ivan Fehrenbach.

Nossack's initial perspective on the firestorm that consumed his native city was from a country cabin that stood about ten miles south of Hamburg's outskirts. Nossack reports that on Wednesday, July 21, 1943, he went there to join his wife, Nisi, who had rented the place for a vacation that might help them, at least for a time, to forget the war. From their country perspective, Nossack reports, a clear day made it possible to see all the way to the city.

The Nossacks' vacation did not last long. There was no escape from the downfall, from the war and its bombs, which brought the smoke, heat, death, and stench that left those who remained "without a center."[2] Only a few days after Nossack had departed Hamburg for his wartime holiday, "the sound of eighteen hundred airplanes" fractured time forever, at least for him.[3] Air raids on Hamburg were nothing new, but when they reached a climax in July 1943, Nossack says, "It was the end."[4]

Shortly returning not only to a devastated Hamburg but also to their ruined world, the Nossacks experienced "the frightening extent to which we have lost touch with everything we once took for granted."[5] Nossack amplifies the irretrievable quality of this loss in his observation that the words *could have* were among the most painful that might be thought or said within the abyss that had once been a priceless German city. *Could have* recalled possibilities, gone forever, that might have produced a reality very different from Hamburg's inescapable misery and the Nazi state that did so much to bring it about. If *could have* suggested how narrowly the Nossacks had escaped death, the phrase also meant that lives did not have to be doomed, wrecked, and violently destroyed. Nevertheless, human decisions — the most crucial ones including those made by Germans themselves — had condemned millions to that fate.

The words *could have* deepened the despair that Nossack may have felt when he remembered a conversation fragment that he overheard one day in Hamburg's anguish. Speaking to her daughter, an old woman said, "Didn't I always tell you, you could have" — and then, says Nossack, "the daughter howled like a mortally wounded animal." He adds that "nowadays, when someone in conversation is on the verge of straying into the realm of 'could have,' someone else will quickly admonish or beg him to stop; or the speaker will notice it himself and abruptly break off, saying: Oh well, it doesn't matter."[6]

The tone of *The Wolves of World War II* is not the same as Nossack's reflections about Hamburg, but it is written in some of the same minor keys. Hans Thiel's moods are less melancholy, his words less poetic, than those of his Hamburg contemporary. Their circumstances were notably different, too — Nossack the city-dwelling novelist, Thiel the farmer whose East Prussian land was far removed geographically and culturally from Nossack's sophisticated urban turf. Nevertheless, these two Germans were linked by more than their shared first name. They are "brothers" who would have understood each other.

As far as I know, Nossack and Thiel never met, but they would have understood one another because they had in common a stance toward Nazism that Fehrenbach aptly calls *troubled resignation*. Both were loyal Germans but by no means dedicated Nazis. While they would stand by their homeland, fighting ferociously for its defense in Thiel's case and profoundly lamenting its destruction in Nossack's, neither of them embedded their hopes in the Nazi cause, nor did they trust the Third Reich's leaders. In multiple ways — patriotically and personally — they were *troubled* Germans.

Nossack and Thiel were troubled because they knew that their nation had gone in directions that were not good. They were troubled because they knew firsthand that the results of Nazism were disastrous. But they were also troubled because they knew that their decisions kept them more on the side of the Nazi regime than in resistance against it. To a considerable extent, no matter how active they were, these two men resigned themselves to an ambiguous existence, to a gray zone. It consisted of being loyal to Germany in Nazi times — times that they might regret and even despise but not to the extent of overt resistance against a government whose *Untergang*, both downfall and end, they could clearly see was coming and, they both acknowledged, was even deserved.

By 1943, Nossack had written numerous works, including plays and poems, but contrary to some reports claiming that the Nazis prohibited him from publishing, any censorship in Nossack's case was more of his own making than imposed upon him by the state. Whatever his personal dislike for Nazism may have been, he was not a vocal opponent of the regime, whose watchfulness found him not to be of great consequence, one way or another, to the Nazi cause. Nossack's negative appraisal of the National Socialism became public well after it was safe and even politically correct to give it.

A parallel pattern can be found in Thiel's case. "Not everyone howled with the wolves," he writes. "Yet to set yourself openly against the current was also impossible, and usually meant the loss of your existence, of your family and of your life." *Impossible* does not ring entirely true; there were Germans who resisted, difficult and life-threatening though such actions surely were. Meanwhile, Thiel appears early on to have welcomed, or at least not to have stridently opposed, significant parts of Nazi agricultural policy, including that policy's exempting him from military service because his farming contributions to the war effort were considered indispensable. That protection, however, did not last. In January 1945, Thiel was drafted into the ragtag and largely hapless *Volkssturm*, a last-ditch "People's Army," its ill-equipped and inadequately trained units consisting of older men and boys, which Hitler desperately deployed to save the Reich. Knowing that he was in a lost cause, one that would cost him his home and threaten his family life, Thiel nevertheless fought with courage and distinction on the Germans' crumbling eastern front, where he and his comrades did all that they could to prevent the dreaded Red Army from bringing about Germany's downfall.

Thiel's readers will discover how agonizing and slow the end was for him. Captured by Russians, imprisoned for years in postwar Poland, frequently beaten and often ill to the point of death along the way, narrowly escaping to the American zone in Allied-occupied Germany, Thiel, "despite his strength," as Fehrenbach's epilogue succinctly puts it, "never completely overcame the physical and emotional wounds caused by the wolves of war."

Troubled resignation was not enough to exempt Thiel completely from participating in the defense of a nation — even if his homeland — ruled by a Nazi regime that was driven by antisemitism, racism, and ethnic discrimination. It also needs to be underscored, however, that Thiel's postwar Polish captors abused him. They did not punish him, at least not justly, because of specific actions he had taken. They abused him because he was German. The abuse that Thiel and some of his German comrades experienced should not be regarded as morally equivalent to the worst atrocities that Nazi Germany inflicted on Jews and Poles, but no atrocity should be passed over in silence, let alone condoned. Thiel's recollections — and arguably Nossack's as well — show that, at least to some extent, Germans were also victims of human rights abuses in World War II and its aftermath.

The rise and fall of the Third Reich cost Thiel more than Nossack. At war's end, Nossack's best days, at least those that included his status as a prize-winning author, were ahead of him. The same cannot be said of Thiel. Probably his happiest times had already been spent on his East Prussian farm well before he experienced combat and captivity on the eastern front. His memoir, written in the late 1940s but left unpolished, was virtually forgotten until Fehrenbach gave it new life more than three decades after Thiel had passed away.

Nossack and Thiel — these different but related Germans linked by troubled resignation — leave at least four troubling questions for their readers. First, why do Nossack and Thiel say so little about the fact that Nazi Germany, in Sebald's words, "murdered and worked to death millions of people in its camps," Jewish losses the greatest in that catastrophe?[7] Hearing of those realities must have complicated their troubled resignation to Nazi Germany.

Second, should Nossack, Thiel, and other Germans akin to them be included among the victims of Hitler and his National Socialism? Arguably, the answer can be — even should be — yes. That answer, however, ought to be carefully qualified, for Nossack and Thiel were by no means victims of the Third Reich in ways equivalent to the Jews and other so-called inferior people who were targeted by Nazi Germany's genocidal antisemitism and racism. Nazism and German troubled resignation toward it did much damage and harm to people such as Nossack and Thiel, who did not choose to be part of the Third Reich and yet found themselves — through their own action or inaction — unable to be anywhere else. Real though it was, their victim status remains ambiguous and must be colored in shades of gray.

Third, while acknowledging their ambiguous status, to what extent were Germans such as Nossack and Thiel victims of human rights abuses that came not only from the policies of Nazi Germany but also, for example, from the Allies' bombers or from postwar Polish captors who mistreated Germans on ethnic grounds? Ethical and political issues about war, justice, punishment, restitution, and revenge are embedded in that vexing question. Versions of their challenges still loom large decades after World War II.

If these foreword assessments are accurate, then the memoirs of Nossack and Thiel raise one more troubling question at the end. It pertains less to them than to those who may read their accounts. Fortunately, the Third Reich no longer exists, but citizens of many nations, including the major powers in the twenty-first century, face a dilemma related to the circumstances in which Nossack and Thiel made their decisions: How will we respond and how should we act when we find ourselves living in a nation headed in directions that are not good? Nossack and Thiel took their paths of troubled resignation. Unavoidably, their readers will evaluate what those men did or did not do. If we listen to them well, the voices of Nossack and Thiel will ask us in return: What would you have done differently? What might you do better now and in the future?

Notes

1. W. G. Sebald, *On the Natural History of Destruction*, trans. Anthea Bell (New York: Random House, 2003), p. 26. The book was originally published in German as *Luftkrieg und Literatur* in 1999.

2. Hans Erich Nossack, *The End: Hamburg 1943*, trans. Joel Agee (Chicago: University of Chicago Press, 2004), p. 31.

3. Ibid., p. 8.

4. Ibid.

5. Ibid., p. 23.

6. Ibid., p. 27.

7. Sebald, *On the Natural History of Destruction*, p. 13.

John K. Roth is Edward J. Sexton Professor of Philosophy and Director of the Center for the Study of the Holocaust, Genocide, and Human Rights at Claremont McKenna College.

Introduction

by Ivan Fehrenbach

Hans Thiel was born in 1902 on a farm near Passenheim, East Prussia, which today is Pasym, Poland. Among the more comfortable families in the region, the Thiels also had a house at a resort area nearby, then named Allenstein, but now known as Olsztyn. Hans was the youngest of seven children; their future occupations ranged from farmer to lawyer to engineer, and their political views on the Third Reich ranged from the committed Nazism of an older brother to Hans' troubled resignation. In time, Thiel married and took over the family farm, which consisted of a flourmill, a sawmill, and wheat fields. A nearby lake served well for family ice-skating during the winter, or boating and swimming in the summer.

In short, life was good. When he was not attending to farm business, Thiel enjoyed outdoor activities with his family, or he went tromping through the nearby forest on hunts. He was a hard and competent worker, and by the time Germany found itself in its second war of the century, he was sufficiently respected in his occupation to be officially classified as "indispensable." For that reason, Thiel remained deployed on the homefront in his capacity as farmer. Nevertheless, he was also labeled by the NSDAP (the Nazi Party) as a possible dissident.

In the first part of the memoir that follows, Thiel writes fragmentarily of this agrarian life during the war. (For a more detailed description of the wartime agricultural arrangement in Germany, in which Thiel's circumstances can be better understood, see Appendix A:

163–164). He also relates various other scenes from the homefront as the war moved closer to East Prussia. But Thiel's memoir primarily covers the war's final year, when he was drafted and served as an active combatant, and the years he was imprisoned following the war.

Conscription and Battle

As the war dragged on, Germany's manpower was gradually being depleted. Everyone at the homefront was forced to take on an increasingly burdensome number of responsibilities. Many elderly farmers, for example, were required to take part in the *Wachdienst*, "the watch service," or the "rural home guard," an organization designed to assist the local authorities. As a successful farmer, Thiel was required to supervise a large number of farms, a task that adversely affected his own farm, "since," as he writes, "[he] was always away." To make matters worse for Thiel and his farm, he was drafted in the summer of 1944 into a labor and construction force activated under the *Volksaufgebot* (The People's Levy), a conscription that the Nazi government created to help regular troops build fortifications in East Prussia. The regular soldiers, as Thiel makes clear, found this collection of varied civilians (controlled by the NSDAP) less than helpful, and those recruited for this labor often found themselves with little work to do.

As the homefront disintegrated, so did the regular army, the *Wehrmacht*. But Hitler refused to consider surrender an option. On September 25th, 1944, he issued a decree forming the *Volkssturm* or "People's Army," something of a home militia devised to bolster the *Wehrmacht* in combat. The *Volkssturm* was activated in October, and like the *Volksaufgebot*, the *Volkssturm* was controlled by the NSDAP and not by the *Wehrmacht*. So as a military arm run by the Nazi Party and administered by the area and district Party leaders (*Gauleiter* and *Kreisleiter*, respectively), the *Volkssturm* was and remained something of an organizational disaster. All remaining able-bodied men who were not already in the military — from the teenagers in the *Hitler Jugend*, to men as old as sixty-five (including those who had previously been classified as "indispensable" to the homefront) — were now subject to being drafted into the *Volkssturm*.

In early January 1945, just a few months after having returned home from the unsuccessful *Volksaufgebot* enterprise (and despite his former status as "indispensable"), Thiel was drafted into the *Volkssturm*. A few days later — on January 13 — the Russians opened their major assault on the Eastern Front. The *Volkssturm* soldiers were supposed to be deployed only in their own districts, but many (including Thiel) wound up on the Eastern Front, where they defended against the invading enemy and helped to evacuate German civilians ahead of the approaching Soviet Army.

Near the end of the war, in the late winter and early spring of 1945, the general mood of the German forces sank rapidly to one of hopelessness and disillusionment. With the *Wehrmacht* itself without sufficient weapons and ammunition, and with the *Volkssturm* not much more than a rag-tag collection of poorly armed youth and the elderly, the German military could barely defend itself against a better-supplied and stronger enemy. It had no hope of mounting any offensive of its own.

While Thiel had no desire to defend the Nazi regime, he nevertheless wanted to help save his people and his land from destruction. With that destruction imminent, the options were few and unattractive. Chaos and anarchy reigned; many of the soldiers went to extremes attempting to return home, including wounding themselves. Thiel himself considers deserting on more than one occasion, and once he even writes of killing himself to prevent the Russians from taking him prisoner.

But he could not, as he writes with his characteristic sardonic humor, allow the Russians to "waltz" into his East Prussian province and "introduce them to our wives." Nor could he allow the enemy to rape and kill women and then burn the town to mask their atrocities. Throughout his time at the front, Thiel confronted many examples of this hell, and he reacted as any decent human being would. In the end, Thiel always considered himself a patriotic German and believed it his responsibility to defend his people. To him, Hitler was not Germany, as the slogan *Hitler ist Deutschland!* claimed.

At the end of the war, Thiel welcomed the allied troops to his country. He hoped that the occupation of these troops would help the Germans regain some sense of honor and decency. His welcome did not, however, extend to the Soviet troops, whom he faced on the Eastern Front. They were the despised Bolsheviks, and, seeking revenge for the Nazi treatment of the Russian population, the Russians were also dreaded as merciless conquerors who brutalized everything German they overran, not just combatants, but civilians (especially women), farm animals, and even graves.

Imprisonment

As he takes pains to note in his memoir, Thiel greatly feared capture by the Russians. This fear was not uncommon, as stories of Russian atrocities were plentiful. Nevertheless, the "hated and feared captivity" became reality on March 28, 1945, when Soviet tanks overran his unit. He was taken prisoner outside of Danzig (now Gdansk), two days before that city fell. Led by his Russian captors on a seemingly purposeless trek through parts of Pomerania, Thiel was released following the cessation of hostilities in May 1945. Or at least he was supposed to be. As Thiel writes in the memoir, the Russians assign him a group of men and tell him to report to a local headquarters. There, he and the other prisoners of war would be put on transports to their homes. At a train-station in Bromberg (now Bydgoszcz), however, the Russians mysteriously disappear, and the prisoners, exhausted and ailing, find themselves under Polish control.

The Poles distribute the prisoners among several Polish-run camps in the region, some of which had housed Poles and Jews imprisoned by the Nazis only days before the Soviet forces reached their gates. The main camp in the region, Potulitz (now Potulice), where Thiel spent much of his imprisonment, began as an assembly camp in 1941 and was run by the SS (*Schutzstaffel*), the elite military organization of the Nazi Party directed by Heinrich Himmler. Potulitz then became a work camp in the summer of 1942, and also served as a sub-camp of the notorious concentration camp, Stutthof, east of Danzig. At the advance of Soviet troops, the SS dissolved the camp on January 20, 1945. A few months later, the Russians took it over, passing it to the Polish secret police in June.

The Polish administration treated its inmates dreadfully — even compared with how the Russian captors treated their inmates. Thiel's status as a prisoner had been a troubling concern for him from the moment of his capture. Since members of the *Volkssturm* were not part of the regular army, and since some of the enemy chose to classify them as civilians (initially, at least, they had no uniforms, only an armband signifying their military status worn with whatever clothes they had brought with them), they were not assured the protections of the Geneva Conventions. Further, when the Soviets burst through the German lines on the Eastern Front, German units disintegrated, and men like Thiel in the *Volkssturm* found themselves attached to and fighting alongside *Wehrmacht* regulars. His ambiguous military status posed serious problems for him as a prisoner of both the Russian and the Polish, but it was during the three years under the Polish authorities that Thiel suffered the most.

During that period, Thiel was abused both mentally and physically, he was sent from one prison to another, he was repeatedly lied to about a fictitious transport home, and he was denied many of the basic necessities of life. When the Polish authorities finally put him on trial, Thiel had already spent one and a half years in prison, during which time he was kept ignorant of his fate and of his captors' intentions. He did not know if he was doomed to live out his days in this hell: barely subsisting on starvation rations, attempting to withstand one torture after another, and wondering if he would ever see his family again.

Even after his conviction by a Polish court, the impartiality of which was questionable at best, none of these questions was answered. The judge refused to state whether Thiel's sentence of three years was in addition to the one and a half years he had already spent in Polish custody, and later, the prison administration even demanded that he pay court costs, though it had made certain that no prisoners entered its walls carrying money or valuables. The torturous, unpredictable camp life continued, and a good part of it was spent in a regular penitentiary with civilian criminals in Konitz (now Chojnice).

For the first year or two, depending on the jail or camp, the Poles did not permit the prisoners in the camps to write or receive letters. Therefore, Thiel did not know for some time whether his family had escaped their home, if they had all survived, or if they were safe. Nor did he know whether they had any idea of his fate. In fact, while Thiel was away at the front and in prison, his wife, two daughters, and young son followed the course of hundreds of thousands of other refugees, fleeing East Prussia in early 1945. They left almost all of their worldly possessions to a throng of toughened Russian soldiers only three kilometers away.

They traveled to Königsberg (Kaliningrad), then to Gotenhafen (Gdynia), and finally embarked on one of the last ships from Gotenhafen to Denmark. (Ironically, Thiel was captured near Gotenhafen outside Danzig a few months later.) After the war, they eventually returned to Germany and moved to Kassel. But the son, Thomas, had died during the escape. When they finally communicate, Thiel learns that all but his son and one brother are alive and well, but he still does not know whether he will ever see his family again or escape his current hell — and a hell it was, for the new Polish camps resembled the Nazi concentration camps more than superficially.

Not only were many of the buildings the same, but a number of the new commandants had also been inmates at the concentration camps during the war. Now these camp authorities subjected the German prisoners to the same forms of torture that recently had killed hundreds of thousands of their own people. Also like the Nazis, the Polish did not stop at physical and mental abuse; Kaltwasser, a camp near Bromberg (Bydgoszcz), was particularly notorious for its mass executions. In late 1945, Kaltwasser was dissolved and its surviving inmates sent to Langenau (Legnowo), a nearby camp where Thiel also spent time. The inmates of Langenau, as with those of all the other nearby camps, eventually went to Potulitz.

The majority of Germans in these camps, like Thiel, were not the perpetrators of Nazi crimes. For the most part, they were non-combatant civilians, and a large number were women and children. A small percentage of the inmates consisted of POWs, some of whom, like Thiel, having fought as last ditch conscripts only to defend their land and families, held no allegiance to Hitler or the Nazis.

Thiel was released from Potulitz with the expectation that he would be allowed to go home, but instead he found himself transported to another prison, this time with civilian criminals, in Konitz (Chojnice). Later he returned to Potulitz, following the same pattern:

hope of release, then reimprisonment. After nearly four years of captivity, Thiel was transported from Poland and released in East Germany. He then found his way to freedom: seizing an opportune chance, Thiel stowed away on a train near the West German border (between Hesse and Thuringia) and crossed over into the American sector.

Even if the Poles and Russians had not prevented his return to East Prussia, Thiel would not have seen his farm again. According to the Potsdam Conference, all Germans forfeited their property and rights and had to move west of a line drawn along the Oder and Neisse rivers. The agreements made by the Allies at Potsdam, however, or anywhere else for that matter, had little effect on a man who watched his Polish master shred the discharge papers given him by his first captors, the Russians, and then scatter the scraps on the ground before him.

Yet despite such trials and horrors, sixty years later, in sharp contrast to the wealth of information on Hitler and the Nazi atrocities, few people know of such events in post-war Poland. Several factors contribute to this scarcity of material, including, perhaps, the fear that critics would view any discussion of abuse of German prisoners, military as well as civilian, as a defense of the Nazis. Concealing or ignoring atrocity, however, whatever its form or wherever it is found, serves neither history nor truth. As Elie Wiesel has said, "Anyone who does not actively, constantly engage in remembering and in making others remember is an accomplice of the enemy (*Dimensions of the Holocaust*, 1977, p. 16).

Finally, as memoirist and as one almost certainly writing for his family to whom he sent the manuscript here translated, Thiel understandably does not provide the documentation that a historian or a journalist would. It is remarkable, however, how the events and scenes described by Thiel are time and again found mentioned in the works by historians writing decades after the incidents occurred and after Thiel writes. Sometimes these are general (e.g., the wasteful use of men drafted under the *Aufsgebot* for fortification work in East Prussia in 1944); but sometimes they are highly particular incidents (e.g., the description of the bodies hanging from trees in Danzig, people killed in retribution, bearing placards marking their offenses; the description of Christmas in the camp at Potulitz. See, e.g., David K. Yelton, *Hitler's*

Volkssturm [2002] and Christopher Duffy, *Red Storm on the Reich* [1991]). These lines of striking continuity demonstrate that Hans Thiel's work serves to open further the eyes of history to events only recently recognized, and it does so with the insight of one who lived those years of horror.

Thiel the Memoirist

Not every reader will react the same way to the events that Thiel describes in his memoir, or for that matter, to the man, Hans Thiel. However, most would probably agree that the tonal range of the memoir, varied and uncontrived, stretching from anger to virtual despair, from fear to sporadic hope, and from disgust to a strange humor, gives the work an authenticity that makes it accessible and even sympathetic. The humor is almost always etched by irony and often touches the level of the sardonic. Perhaps this dark drollery is related to the character of his audience as much as to the character of the author. The audience, after all, was almost certainly thought by Thiel to be limited to his family, and perhaps only to his brother to whom he sent the memoir as something akin to a long letter. Such a document carries with it a certain honesty born of the writer's familiarity and intimacy with its recipient, allowing, among other things, the personal to be expressed without embarrassment.

A few patterns of Thiel's behavior, as presented in the memoir, capture special attention. One is Thiel's repeated attempts to avoid being given positions of authority by those in command. His attempts could be simple self-effacement, while they could also be seen as a reluctance to take on positions of responsibility with the potential for later reproach, even perhaps recrimination. That such authority nonetheless was repeatedly thrust upon him can be attributed in part to his comparative vigor, his obvious managerial experience, and even his impressive stature — at six foot four inches Thiel was an imposing figure. And in the *Volkssturm*, for example, Thiel, in his mid forties, was among many who were sexagenarians on the one hand and teenagers from the *Hitler Jugend* on the other.

In addition, Thiel repeatedly speaks of his remarkable luck in escaping many bad situations, but occasionally he seems to attribute his survival to impressive cunning and fortitude instead of luck, portraying his actions more as courageous leadership than good fortune. The two explanations create a strange incongruity, the emphasis on luck revealing a certain modesty and humility that perhaps saved him; as he writes, "It was said that they never knew what to do with me; they couldn't find any reasons to attack me." On the other hand, the depictions of boldness or invincibility, for example his insistence that no one has touched him and "No one will [touch me] and go unpunished," convey a contrasting immodesty. A strange juxtaposition, though not inexplicable, for perhaps this peculiar union of traits reveals Thiel's own difficulty in understanding how he managed to exist and, in the end, to survive amidst the different wolves that appear in time of war. Taken as a whole, however, what Thiel has left us suggests that his survival, as with so many others in like circumstances, depended less on his outwitting, much less on his overwhelming the wolves of war than on his outlasting them until he found himself free — if not at true peace.

The ironic and often dark humor, seen especially in his many metaphors that set the deed against the words that describe it, may reflect an unconscious device used by Thiel as a defense against the horrors that he experienced and then describes. Among these peculiar, oddly humorous descriptions is a passage previously cited: He was not going to allow the Russians to "waltz" into his country and "introduce them to our wives." And then there are the many times he refers to bullets and other deadly missiles as "gifts" from the enemy. On the appearance of the motley garb of the *Volkssturm*: "A robber baron would have been quite delighted by our varied and colorful troops." On the carnage of battle: "we see wounded men helping each other, and then the dead, who no longer need help," and on four men he found dead with their meal before them, "the four men there wouldn't be eating for a long time." On the invigorating character of battle: "Heavy chunks of earth whistled by our ears; old legs became amazingly agile." And then there is his jaundiced comment on the location of the prison in Konitz: "peculiar, that prisons almost always stand wall to wall with a place of worship." And after commenting on the Party officials driving around in big cars "with spruced-up whores," Thiel writes with authentic gallows humor: "Though we should have, no one dared shoot up the tires of those vehicles — court martials are handed out quickly — you only had to search out the tree." These passages and images manage to capture the complexity and confusion of such events in a way that straightforward descriptions could not — even when (indeed, especially when) they are at odds with what is being described.

The Manuscript and the Translation

The Thiel manuscript, a cramped, single-spaced typescript of eighty-six pages, remained virtually untouched for almost fifty years after Thiel's brother, August Thiel, received it in the United States. A few people had perused it; some attempted to translate it, but all such attempts were short-lived, and the manuscript ran the distinct danger of disintegrating in a hot Virginia attic. As a friend of the Thiel family, I had heard of the memoir, and while studying literary translation at Brown University, I remembered it and inquired about it. It was again exhumed and the brittle pages came into my hands before time made reading them impossible.

One of the reasons other translation attempts came to naught was that the manuscript posed some special problems for translation. Thiel often uses words that differ from their current German usage, and some of his vocabulary has fallen out of use entirely, except perhaps in certain dialects. In other cases, Thiel tries to transcribe Russian or Polish words, often misspelling them and making recognition extremely difficult. A knowledge of the keyboard proved invaluable in figuring out some words. Mistakes such as "*ost*," which means "east," instead of "*ist*," which means "is," were common.

Moreover, Thiel's intentions for the manuscript are unclear. His manuscript was obviously not a final draft, if he ever intended to have a final draft. Even the German that is recognizable to a modern reader is often difficult to read because of misspellings and places where he has typed several letters in one space. There are numerous other typographical errors and a number of faulty transitions — Thiel often changes his topic mid-sentence. Sentence fragments with missing subjects, along with erratic shifts in tense, often posed considerable difficulties for translation. Some of these stylistic defects have been silently emended, but many — in particular, numerous abrupt tense shifts — have been left as they appear in the manuscript. Correcting all would have seriously altered the character of the memoir as Thiel wrote it.

The reader should be alerted to the particular problems of structure and expression found at the beginning of the memoir when Thiel is writing about life prior to his being drafted into the *Volkssturm*. Identified in the current translation as "Part I: A Picture of the Homefront," that section presented the greatest challenge for translation, fraught as it is with more than its proportionate share of problems of clarity and coherence. There is no way to know for certain why this is the case. Perhaps, however, Thiel's treating so many different subjects and his need to shift frequently in time and place in this section may explain why this part's structure is loose and its narrative often diffuse. Thiel's narrative becomes noticeably sharper and more focused and his description richer and more vigorous as soon as he begins describing his experiences after departing the homefront for combat.

Thiel often uses abbreviations, especially for locations (see Appendix B "Thiel's Sojourn" pp. 165–170), and makes almost no use of any organizational techniques such as headings or paragraphs. He sometimes adds a few extra spaces between sentences, but almost all organizational arrangements as they exist in the text that follows are mine, including the section titles, headings and notes, which were introduced to facilitate coherence and to provide the reader with direction. Words and phrases in parentheses are Thiel's; words and phrases in square brackets are editorial emendations. Thiel's numbers, however, remain throughout as he wrote them, sometimes spelled out, sometimes in numerical form.

The manuscript made it to the United States directly. August Thiel had moved to America before the war, and he sometimes assisted Hans after the war by sending packages and money. Hans sent the manuscript to August not long after his return from imprisonment, some time around 1948–9. Perhaps the manuscript was an explanation to his brother of what Thiel had gone through, of why, for example, he had been writing him for money from a Polish prison.

Other than the organizational changes, I have attempted to remain as faithful to the original as possible. Where my translation does not literally convey the German original, I believe and hope that I have managed to be faithful to the general sense and meaning intended by Thiel, for it is important that the particular experience of Hans Thiel be known and remembered.

Top left: Hans Thiel, 1928. *Top right:* Thiel and one of his daughters, 1932. *Bottom:* Thiel hunting with his brother Franz before the war.

Top: Hans Thiel with his sister-in-law and nephew. *Bottom:* The Thiel villa in Passenheim.

Not everyone howled with the wolves, and only an unscrupulous person could do so. Yet to set yourself openly against the current was also impossible, and usually meant the loss of your existence, of your family and of your life.... There were effective methods of getting the best and greatest effort from each Volk *comrade.... The comrade was always between a rock and a hard place. A pistol was at his chest, as it were — he did as they wanted, or else.*

— Hans Thiel

I

A Picture of the Homefront[1]

Summer 1944: The harvest in our old East Prussian province was close to ripe, and on the average it promised to be good. If the workers, machines and fuel remained sufficiently at our disposal, and if St. Peter didn't become too unfriendly, we farmers could consider the crop (in the sense of the "homefront")[2] as a battle one hundred percent won. The same favorable reports came from the remaining parts of Germany. The few of us who had remained — that is, those whom the *Reichsnährstand*[3] allegedly believed it needed in order to keep the people fed — faithfully completed the harvest, despite facing endless difficulties.

We happily did without the promised "help" of the troops who were distributed among the cities and towns — experience from past years had taught us that this "relief" sometimes came in the form of a burden. The relationship between the rural population and the troops was not always friendly, for the typical soldier (whom I'm discussing here) had spent time — maybe a long time, maybe a short

1. As noted in the introduction on p. 17, this first section of the memoir is particularly diffuse and even, at times, difficult to follow. This problem might be because in describing the atmosphere on the homefront, Thiel attempts to cover a wide variety of loosely connected subjects. His narrative becomes noticeably sharper when he takes up the events of life in combat and captivity, beginning in Part II.

2. *Erzeugungsschlacht* is translated as "homefront," but the word has additional connotations associated with the Nazi domestic policy.

3. The *Reichsnährstand* was an agricultural program instituted by the Nazis to aid the German farmer. For a more complete discussion of this program, see Appendix A, "A Note on Agrarian Policy and Farm Life Under the Third Reich," on pages 163–164.

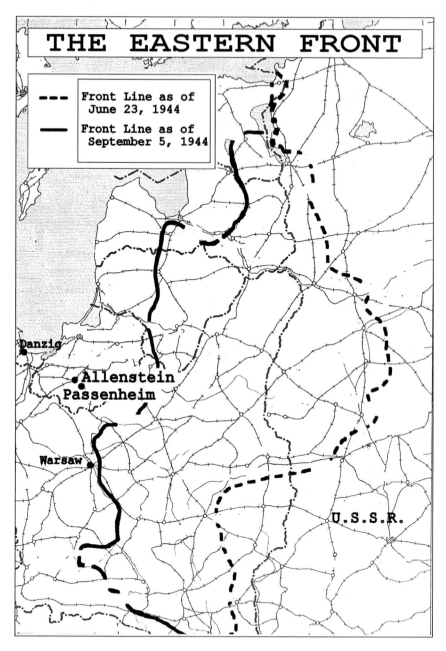

THE EASTERN FRONT

- - - Front Line as of
      June 23, 1944

——— Front Line as of
      September 5, 1944

Danzig

Allenstein
Passenheim

Warsaw

U.S.S.R.

The Eastern Front, July–September, 1944. The front line moved swiftly during
the summer months of 1944, and by September the Soviet Army had driven deeply
into East Prussia. The *Volkssturm* was created by Hitler in late September in an
attempt to halt that assault. The Thiel family had homes in both Allenstein and
Passenheim. From a map by the Office of Strategic Services.

time — at some front, had been wounded and assigned to a reserve unit through a military hospital, and was now awaiting new orders to return to the front. It was, of course, understandable that he wanted to enjoy this last respite to its utmost, and that he got as far as possible from every activity that smelled at all of work — but he was hardly any help with the harvest.

The resident families of farmers could no longer help either, except for those few clever men here and there (or those with good though expensive connections) who managed to be held back from the front. These few men were the only people we had to help train the foreign workers for the necessary jobs, and indeed the only ones to help carry on business at all.

The apartment buildings were crowded (and for the most part overcrowded) with women and children who had been evacuated from the bombed central and western German cities. Everyone was nervous. Daily life was complete chaos.

We were most irritated by the old resident families whose men were in the war or killed in action. These women and their adolescent children wouldn't lift one damned finger, and so they often made our blood boil. The state threw so much support money at these women that they could live off it — and royally. Why, then, should they do more than what absolutely had to be done, such as the most necessary house cleaning? We watched as these previously hard-working and simple-living women, fortified by the help of the *L. Schein*[4] (agricultural — eggs, butter, bacon, poultry, etc.), were suddenly seen out buying themselves new clothes and bicycles. And soon they could only be found on their way to the hairdresser or the movie theater.

A work requirement of thirty hours per week was introduced but unfortunately never consistently enforced, and it was hardly ever observed. You heard one of the frequent, well-tested excuses: there was laundry to do, or bread to bake, or a sickness, or children to get, or bad weather, etc., and if in one or another exceptionally bad case, a department head was asked, or forced, to take drastic measures,

4. "L." stands for *landwirtschaftlicher* which translates as "agricultural." A *Schein* is a bill or banknote. Thus, the "L." Schein is the term used to refer to the food-stamp-like allotments given to people during the war.

then for the following month the women vowed to improve — while they continued to lounge about.

The men at the various fronts managed to send packages to their families, or have them delivered, from Sweden, Norway, Finland, Denmark, Romania, France, Holland, Italy, etc. with things that these men would never have been able to acquire otherwise. It was possible to look at the children or women and know with certainty where their relatives were deployed.

At this time, life was not all that bad. The bombs had not yet fallen (the Russian was too poor of a pilot) apart from small, single strikes on Königsberg or Elbing, or on an important piece of railway in one place or another. The strictly demanded blackouts were considered bothersome and unnecessary.

The only problem was that there were so few things to buy. Money was really only good for those things that weren't rationed, but everything was rationed. Alcohol and tobacco were especially scarce. But here and for other things, the *L. Schein* helped us to make do.

At that time the farmer was aptly referred to as: "*Erbhofbauer* — by Hitler's grace." It was fitting, for due to Hitler's laws, the *Erbhofbauer* enjoyed such times as were unknown before the Third Reich. Anyone who had a plot of land from 7.5 to 125 hectares qualified as an *Erbhofbauer*, but every once in a while larger operations (mine was larger) could obtain the *Erbhof* status by way of a special exception. The owners of such farming operations were either one hundred percent Nazis, or they had managed in some other way to make themselves useful to the Party, in art, or science, or something similar (I also failed this test).

In any case, because of the law and the privileges conferred to every qualifying farmer, these particular operations were practically guaranteed success. So it was no surprise that after years of this "fat life," the owners had lost all taste for work. Receiving large amounts of support money, having debts forgiven, and last but not least utilizing cheap foreign workers, all allowed the farmer to live the so-called "high life." And unfortunately, in many cases, he quickly grew accustomed to this lush and reckless lifestyle.

So the old simple field wagon and the good Sunday wagon had

made room for an automobile, which, however, was now rusting in the corner of the shed because of fuel shortages. So the farmer was left to remember a grand and trouble-free time that had disappeared much too quickly. There had been many merry and unnecessary drives, with that fender and that brimming wallet going straight to hell.

Life was good then if you were an *Erbhofbauer*; he furnished himself with a "party member number," became an automobile owner, and wasted the least amount of time as possible working in the yard or in the field. Thus he could become a more regular caller at the town hall offices and at the offices of the Party. There was a certain sense of "fatness" always surrounding around him, and the most important requirement didn't cost him anything and became easy after years of practice — just saying a pointed "*Heil* Hitler" whenever appropriate.[5]

The *Erbhof* farmers had already become faithful followers of the *Führer*, as was the labor force as a whole, for the workers had nothing at all to complain about. From the deepest part of their hearts they prayed to their dear Lord that the atmosphere would remain just as it was. When Adolf petitioned the people with his innumerable appeals, such as, "I am addressing my most faithful, the workers and the farmers...," he spoke the absolute truth. Both the workers and the farmers could happily agree with both him and his regime.

It would hardly be interesting to say anything more about the *Erbhof* laws here. I was warned several times to hold my tongue, by prominent department heads from the NSDAP[6] and by the department of the *Reichsnährstand*. I knew that if I continued to proceed as I did, the keepers of the black list, on which I would remain for a long time as "disagreeable critic," would make sure that someone "got rid of me."[7]

That procedure worked in the following way: first, the revocation of management privilege. Then the collection of (that is, the

5. All official business commenced and ended with this official Nazi salutation.
6. The *Nationalsozialistische Deutsche Arbeiterpartei*, the National Socialist German Workers' Party, the Nazis.
7. *Gashahn abdreht*, literally, "turn off the gas valve."

loss of) the business or the farm, and then you would have been held in custody while the trial was pending. Next you would go to the KZ (concentration camp),[8] and if you were fortunate, it would all come to a quick end in some welcome accident. A small newspaper notice would tell the survivors that Mr. X had been injured, due to a certain act of resistance, or during an attempted escape.

In such circumstances, you had to approach the events with resignation in order to avoid frustration. An intervention, or any kind of judicial ruling, was seldom obtained. And if it was, 9 times out of 10 the result only further disheartened the depressed petitioner.

Neither was it extraordinary if some harmless citizen's workshop, or, for example, a factory producing sausages, cans, shoes or machine tools caught the eye of some distinguished and "honorable" Party member. And how did he go about owning it? Very simply. The shopkeeper or the person in charge was suddenly under investigation, without any apparent reason. The investigators talked with the employees or the house staff, and if they wanted to, they could always find some kind of "violation." There were proceedings, but hardly legal proceedings, for they were performed by the "Labor Front" and the "Labor Trustees," who expediently denied the owner all his management responsibilities and — see above. As a result, a suitable man would have to be found to carry on the business. He was searched for (he had already been ready for some time), and simply appointed or enfeoffed.[9]

In situations such as these, it took a lawyer with guts to represent the interests of the ruined man, for as a rule, a lawyer got the "sign" at the beginning of the trial, warning him to refuse the case. The claim often followed standard lines: the lawyer was told that the case dealt solely with political interests, and that these issues were easily settled outside of the courtroom. Having been told this, some lawyers "understood," while others (of these there were few) had backbones and a good relationship with some uncorrupted office. With such connections a good lawyer could destroy even a

---

8. The German word for "concentration camp" is *Konzentrationslager*, abbreviated as both KZ and KL.

9. Rewarded with a piece of land, as a fief in the Middle Ages.

Gauleiter,[10] provided that he was perfectly certain of his case and that the situation warranted such measures.

The Göring department[11] was well known and managed to remain clean until the end. There was only one instance here that I will mention, because it was typical of the general proceedings. I was able to learn about this case and to follow it rather closely, for we knew the Berlin lawyer[12] very well.

For reasons such as those described above, a west German shoe factory owner was imprisoned under lock and key. His wife was able to contact this lawyer from Berlin, who then, as an old assault corps leader from 1914–18, completely disregarded the "sign." After he had convinced himself of the untenable nature of the charge, he decided, without regard for his own person or practice, to represent the interests of the factory owner.

He flew to the western–German district capital where the man was being held, and even there shrugged off the pressing "signs." He had to argue his way through to the owner's cell, and then, somehow, he managed to be left alone with the man. Back to Berlin and back to the *Gauleitung*. And again the same thing. It became a battle between the all-powerful *Gauleitung* and a lawyer. The Göring department issued commands that not even a *Gauleitung* could reject, and the factory owner was set free, indebted to the lawyer for his life and his existence.

The factory owner's fault: his inherited million-mark business somehow disturbed a Party member or some general Party plans. Or, it was possible that it had merely caught the greedy eye of some Party big shot. As I described above, it was not hard under those circum-

---

10. A *Gau* was the largest administrative region of the Nazi Party, and the *Gauleiter* was in charge of this region. The *Gauleiter* exercised enormous power, and each was appointed by Hitler.

11. Göring department: The terms Thiel uses interchangeably in this phrase (freely translated here as "department") are *Ministerium* and *Dienststelle*. Given the context, Thiel is probably not referring to Hermann Göring's role as head of the *Reichluftfahrtministerium* (Reich Aviation Ministry). If he is referring to that same Hermann Göring, it is probably to the Nazi leader's position as the powerful director of the German economy and industry, in particular in his capacity as director of the *Reichswerke Hermann Göring*. That agency played an important role in the Nazis' Four Year Plan to rearm and become self-sufficient. This plan began in 1936, but the associated projects continued until the Nazis fell.

12. This was apparently one of Thiel's brothers. Why he does not mention that here is unclear; perhaps the political atmosphere was still too uncertain at the time of writing.

stances to find reasons to eliminate an elderly owner, and the justifications were always discovered in the same ways. In his case, for example, the owner had employed two female apprentices from the factory to come to his villa once a week to help his wife with the cleaning. Since only two people lived there, however, his household could not officially employ any help. Furthermore, it was charged that he had raped his female workers (as a kind old man he had generously and frequently taken women and girls to or from work on his trips to the factory), and for these reasons they had denied his ability to run a business. But this man was lucky. In the end he could only complain about the loss of a few valuable machines — during the short period of his arrest they had been dismantled and taken to be used somewhere else.

In contrast to the manufacturing industry, the agricultural industry didn't have to endure such situations on a regular basis. Among other cases, a well known, successful farmer (and dissident) was supposed to lose his position because he had been too good to his Russian prisoners. He had allowed them to have their own church services, for which the poor bastard even found an old Russian noblewoman trained in the orthodox rites, and so on. Furthermore, because of his sharp, candid criticisms and his consciously defiant behavior, he had too often and too strongly enraged the overseeing *Gau* and *Kreisleitungen*.[13]

He had to disappear, and one day to this end the "green Minna" (the police van) appeared beneath his window. Luckily, the wanted man was the first to see the vehicle, and by way of a secret staircase he was able to reach the park and make off. For almost a year the *Gestapo*[14] had a warrant out for him but could never find him (which already means something to one familiar with the conditions of the time). And what had this man done? He was a practicing lawyer and before 1933 an undersecretary of state, head and shoulders above the rabble around him.[15]

---

13. A *Kreis* was another region similar to the *Gau*, but much smaller and the leader less powerful. It was similar to a county.

14. The infamous Nazi State's secret police.

15. It seems that he was a lawyer in addition to owning a farm (or before owning the farm), unless Thiel has accidentally conflated two people. The year 1933 is when Hitler came to power.

One Herr von R. lived close to the lion's jaws, in Potsdam. He found a lawyer (the lawyer I mentioned before), with whom he was able to discuss the concerns of this fugitive, his cousin, von B. He and the cousin remained in constant contact, and von R. wanted to represent him (and was authorized to do so). But for understandable reasons the cousin could not resurface, for were he found again, he would be risking an "accident" while on the transport.

This time, events moved extremely slowly, simply because the wanted man was still remembered as a principal troublemaker from the time of the first coup attempt (at the beginning of the Hitler government). But things proceeded, and again they ended up in the Göring department. Herr von R. helped the lawyer with his affairs and difficulties and became an almost permanent visitor and guest. The arrest warrant was finally cancelled, and all the necessary precautions were taken so that Herr von B. could safely leave his hiding place. But where had he been? He had been visiting Berlin regularly as virtually a daily guest of the lawyer, who nearly fell from his chair when Herr von R. introduced himself as the wanted Herr von B.

Because my farming operation produced and delivered well beyond the customary levels, and perhaps also for other reasons, an honorary but highly undesirable position was forced upon me in my professional *Nährstand*[16] group. As a U.K. man (indispensable[17] — and could not be drafted into the *Wehrmacht*), I was, of course, repeatedly roped into duties. So, for the majority of the week, authorized with certain powers, I was regularly on the move from operation to operation, intervening where things weren't running as they should and uncovering the operations that, for particular reasons, didn't run at all (and required immediate attention).

On these trips — which negatively affected my own business in the long run, since I was always away — I made some very interesting observations that once again turned out to my disadvantage. Simply put, the authorities were unable to convert me. My half-hearted, indifferent sympathy for a system growing more and more insane

---

16. *Nährstand* groups were agricultural groups.
17. *Unabkömmlich*, abbreviated U.K.

sank rapidly to zero. It was often enough to make you sick, but not something you could change. Corruption, wretched brown-nosers and other careerists were everywhere. Upstarts, who in most cases were equipped with neither knowledge nor ability, much less a halfway decent character, sat in the chief places of the most important branches of the economy, solely as the result of their high or low Party status. Some typical guy who wouldn't have attracted a single glance in normal life concealed himself in a dapper uniform. It was a science in itself to recognize and classify with approximate accuracy the innumerable uniforms, the badges of rank, and the insignias.

Now and again these business trips also led me to that part of the eastern region that we occupied.[18] Here, corresponding to the region's vastness and the population's unconditional obedience, the administrative force wasn't as heavy-handed as it was in our own region; nevertheless, circumstances there were the same. Our little gravediggers of the Third Reich didn't miss any opportunity to undermine the good reputation of the German people, to make themselves as hated as possible, and to fill their pockets in the process.

An example: after a few hundred horses and their owners were brought together by the police department to a centrally located point, I had the task of sizing up all of the animals, classifying them, and determining the purchase value of each. Then I arranged the assorted animals, gave them numbers and sent them on a westerly march, where they were distributed to farms on my list along with the certificates with my price quotation. These farms had been weakened due to the oppressive expropriations of the *Wehrmacht*, or because of accidents or something else, and therefore were way behind with the daily fieldwork. Everything seemed in order. Payment was made by the German farmers according to the amounts I determined. The money went to the department in charge, which, for its part, had already advanced the sums to be paid (because this department had the administrative authority in the regions, it also had to pay the suppliers of the horses).

18. Probably the sections of Poland that Germany occupied after carving up the Polish state with the Soviet Union at the beginning of the war.

It was paid in the following manner: I brought the equivalent value of about 170 animals, and had the relevant sales receipts for them in my pocket, minus the settlement and reductions made for the administrative office in the area. At the presentation of the animals, the farmers had needed to state their name and place of residence, which were allegedly recorded in a book. It was more than obvious, to me anyway, that the poor and intimidated Polish farmer hardly dared stammer his name, and if he did, he could never possibly be understood in the reigning chaos. So appearances were kept up. Lists were compiled. The police department took care of the order. But the money never ended up where it was supposed to.[19]

In later years, from all classes of Polish people, and from the mouths of the ethnic Germans as well, from the Volga region, the Ukraine, White Russia, Galicia, etc. I confirmed things that we had heard, but which we only dared discuss in the narrowest circles of friends. The *Landser*,[20] and, therefore, the initial military force and administration, was happily greeted by everyone — and joyfully accepted. But the Party machine that came afterwards was universally condemned, and was tolerated with horror.

Not everyone howled with the wolves, and only an unscrupulous person could do so. Yet to set yourself openly against the current was also impossible, and usually meant the loss of your existence, of your family and of your life. Whoever possessed knowledge and ability was simply named an honorary deputy in his particular field, and woe to whoever attempted to shake off that straitjacket given him. There were effective methods of getting the best and greatest effort from each *Volk* comrade. They had the means to make him a malleable work tool, and as I have explained, they were pretty damned free in using those means. The comrade was always between a rock and a hard place. A pistol was at his chest, as it were — he did as they wanted, or else.

The soldier at the front lived better, even though he was forced every hour to reckon with an ascent to the other world. He was, at

19. Thiel's point, it seems, is that the administrative office (and thus the bureaucrats) ended up with the money that the Polish farmers were supposed to receive for providing the animals by advancing the money to themselves.
20. A *Landser* is a common soldier.

least, spared the whole nerve-racking humdrum of life back where we were. He always passed his vacation at home happily, but in the circle of his comrades, he felt better. The hinterland's control and supervision must have been foreign and incomprehensible to him, especially since not even his family, in the most private parts of its life, remained unmonitored. A mother and housewife, for example, had to go to her meeting, a talk, or a course of instruction at eight o'clock in the morning. The son, a pupil in a H.J.'s uniform,[21] had to do his service somewhere else at the same time, alongside his similarly uniformed and equally obligated sister. Meanwhile, insofar as they couldn't yet be trained, the little buzzing trousers under six years old (luckily, they did not have to wear uniforms) were looked after by loving old relatives or neighbors.

Thus it passed. There were occasional variations, but for years the result was the same — the younger generation treated in this way grew estranged too early; it went wild, acknowledged neither God nor the devil, let alone any parental or educational authority.

A *Sekundaner*[22] of a certain institution was called to answer to a juvenile court because of some cellar-burglaries, which he, the leader, committed with his group of other pupils about the same age. The boy's father was obligated to be at the hearing, where the following exchange took place:

"Your age?"

"56 years old."

"Occupation?"

"Postal employee."

"Children?"

"The oldest son, a soldier — highly decorated and a promising career. One daughter, married, the son-in-law a highly ranked civil servant, also at the front. And then this one here."

"And how is it possible that the accused youngster has failed so horribly?"

The despondent old man couldn't refrain from saying, "The other children were raised by my wife and me; this one here was

---

21. *Hitler Jugend* were those in the "Hitler Youth" programs.
22. A *Sekundaner* was a pupil of the sixth or seventh year of grammar school.

raised by you." It was too bad he said that, for it turned out to be his misfortune. Result? Disciplinary action and dismissal from his office without pension.

Early on, the state took over rearing of the youth. Vocational training, however, still required a private teacher, and without being interviewed or even asked, I was named to what was commonly known as the state *Lehrbetrieb*[23] — with the responsibility to instruct apprentices. For years I succeeded in preventing such apprentices from being assigned to me, using every possible excuse, and thus I avoided a great deal of anger and inevitable anxiety. Quite a few trade school operations were placed on a black list because of their apprentices, in whose ranks were often placed stool pigeons and other informants. As a member of an examining board, I periodically had to take part in some trade school events, and it was often more than I could handle not to get completely enraged, especially when something like the following happened.

One time in a *Bannführer's*[24] concluding speech (he was nineteen to twenty years old), he explained to his collected crowd of devoted, attentive youths, all between sixteen and eighteen: "You no longer need to work as your fathers have worked. You should all become leaders of your own businesses. You already have plenty foreign workers at your disposal, and when the war is finally at an end you will get even more!" With these and similar injections the younger generation of 1940 was molded and shaped, and everything was judged to be in the best of order. It was impossible to enlighten such a gold-tassled prophet, and, at any rate, you could not allow yourself to enter into a debate. These young *Führers* were trained by the Nazi schools, and then they were let loose on all of the poor Germans, in this case on the youth —

To be fair, there is another side to the story. One could not deny that as a result of thorough training, there were extraordinary successes in the fields of health and athletics. In contrast to earlier times, the search for gifted youngsters truly resulted in identifying

23. The state-run trade school.
24. One of the youth-group leaders.

those who were gifted — even those who were poor. The guiding principle "*Frei Bahn dem Tüchtigen!*"[25] was not an empty phrase.

The training of the girls was just as good, even if you had to overlook a few extremes in the enforcement of orders. The important businessman's well-cared for and well-kept daughter had to complete her year of duty just as the lowest worker's daughter did — by helping a farmer who had a lot of children, or by working for a manual laborer or a blue-collar worker, where she had to perform every task presented to her. For everyone concerned, it proved to be an excellent opportunity to learn about each other, an experience that was certainly valuable in their later lives.

The future soldier, free-thinking academic professional, or stiff civil servant without imagination — all were affected just as positively by fulfilling their required time and their labor service. The boys received instruction in discipline and were kept on a damned short leash, and not only was the vocation of one's own father taught, but also how to use the axe, the spade, the hoe, the saw, the hammer, and all the other work tools that formed blisters and calluses. They were also confronted with sound athletic activities, both easy and difficult, and it didn't hurt anyone. And as for a young woman of good standing and birth, it certainly didn't hurt her to learn something new either. And in the end, a tender, spoiled youth had become a real man.

To understand the situation at that time, and to judge what followed that year, it's necessary to describe our surroundings. It's also important to say something about the foreigners who lived with us. There were prisoners of war, civilian prisoners, and internees or "*Hiwi*" (volunteers).[26] Everyone without exception (so long as he was willing to work and wasn't a scoundrel, saboteur, or unpleasant prophet) was treated well, cared for, and paid, regardless of what country he called home.

Perhaps every once in a while in a mass reception camp, where

---

25. A Nazi phrase often translated as "Let ability win through!"

26. See the Glossary as well as Christopher Browning, *Ordinary Men: Reserve Police Battalion 101 and the Final Solution in Poland* (New York: Aaron Asher Books, 1992). Among other issues, Browning discusses these *Hilfswillige*.

the camp administration was all but worthless, or where one inmate or another had done something wrong, an ordinary incident temporarily turned into an unpleasant event. Today some horror stories about concentration camps are still exaggerated and blown out of proportion — unless, and I'm not in a position to know first-hand, it is a matter of the Jewish prisoners. This most disturbing of all the German chapters was not written by the people. By the people it was condemned, rejected. Much more could be said about this.

In general, the foreigner prisoners had no cause to complain, and when one considers the standard of living we had at the time, it must be said that the prisoners didn't live any worse than we did. Years later, I would have happily taken the pieces of bread that these prisoners threw away, for when I was imprisoned, it would have been a feast to receive those remnants that went to the pigs.

Tobacco never ran out. Even at harvest time when the work was pressing, the eight-hour day was the rule, though it often had to be lengthened. But if overtime was taken, the workers were paid extra and were brought additional tobacco, beer or something else. Everyone had a clean bed with a straw mattress, two wool blankets, two towels, a washbowl, soap, eating utensil, etc. and the employer had to provide these materials and make sure they were always there.

Military guards were responsible for clothing the prisoners of war. For the civilian prisoners, the authorities distributed appropriate clothing, which could then be bought, and there were no prisoners without shoes — or a coat — if it was at all possible. Wages came according to set rates, and in many cases prisoners were paid more. Some men didn't spend all their wages, and then with remittance payments, they managed to support relatives at home in France, or some other place.

I was assigned people from different nations one after another, and got along with all of them well. Within this constant flow of twenty or so men I came upon the widest range of social positions and professional classes possible, and I gladly seized every opportunity to talk with them, honestly, even privately over a cigarette. Time and again I came to realize that the so-called hostility between our peoples was nothing more than a product fashioned by a small number of crazed administrators and diplomats, who were unable to lead our peoples to any mutual understanding without a battle-field.

The Italian stood with the Russian or the Pole, the Frenchman, the Belgian, the Dutchman, the Englishman, the German — together they rolled and smoked their last cigarettes, and slapped one another on their shoulders with satisfaction. Perhaps they needed a light, but certainly no referee. All of these different men from different nations worked together, and — provided troublemakers were absent — I never once saw any outbursts of hatred.

I chose to keep a French prisoner of war to help me with the household and the garden. After he had done his service faultlessly for over four years, an opportunity arose whereby I could release him to return home, and when I asked if he would like to leave, expect-ing a joyful eagerness to finally go home, the man instead was crest-fallen and said, "If you don't really want to let me go, then I will stay here with you in Germany forever, and if Herr Chef[27] wants to give me an apartment, then I will also have my wife come here with me."

In the space of his years here, the good Louis[28] had kept his eyes open, and he often couldn't seem to keep his opinions to him-self. "France," he said so often, "is very good for the capitalist. Ger-many, on the other hand, is the best for the worker — and I'll never again find a boss like you, who cares so well for his workers." Natu-rally the latter was something of an exaggeration, but then he often took things a little too far.

When we were out for the evening, he would make himself comfortable with his newspaper or his flute together with "Alf," the truest of all hunting dogs, and he would sit in the hall near the chil-dren's bedroom (we chose him over the less dependable German women we had as personnel), watching the sleeping children until our return. He had his room in the house, and he was always at hand; he was the most dependable attendant and watchman one could hope for.

And then I think back on the Russians, who never would have hit an animal, who never would have let my girls come near even the

27. *Chef* translates roughly as "boss."
28. Louis was the name, like "Joe" for Americans, given to a Frenchman.

38

calmest of horses in the stables, even if they requested it. And to prevent them from doing it, the Russians would entertain them with any type of nonsense — but they acted like real human beings,[29] and had a reputation for being willing, good-natured, and clumsy oafs. And I remember again how my Russians behaved towards the children....

The workers' houses lay close to the estate, and nearby was the lake with its dangerously steep, sloping shores, which in the summer was the children's favorite playground. Here the most dependable guardians were the Ivans,[30] who anxiously kept an eye on the romping bands of children, and who often came to me begging that I tell them to stay out of the water because — "child not able to swim and then go under and then dead. Pan Chef not good if not forbid this game."

In occasional off-duty conversations, they talked freely and without shyness, but they invariably revealed a childishly naive understanding of and attitude towards political issues. They could all read and write, but only a few were capable of even closely grasping concepts such as capitalism, communism or bolshevism. In fact, they had no idea of where to start with these things at all, even though they had all gone to school and had learned to write, calculate, and read maps. To them Russia was an abstraction; it made their eyes light up, and they raved about the huge, rich country. Names like Lenin, Trotsky and Stalin were indeed familiar, yet they mentioned them in the same tone that they spoke about a czar from some earlier time. In any case they knew, and didn't try to hide, that those men wanted only "to possess." No one had brought anything good to the little *muschik*,[31] and whatever any particular "czar" had planned was entirely foreign to them, and moreover, didn't interest them at all. Outside of eating, drinking, and smoking they had hardly any needs. But these men had been lucky: they were taken prisoners of war, unhurt and healthy, and here they were kept well.

29. The German word here is *Mensch*, and the English language lacks an equivalent, but "human being," in the moral and compassionate sense, comes close.

30. Ivan was the slang name, like "Louis" for the Frenchman or "Joe" for Americans, given to the Russian soldier.

31. A farmer or peasant in czarist Russia.

At the beginning of July the telephone rang; it was very late in the day. I am told: "You must appear tomorrow morning at an extremely important internal conference, in the department of the K.C.,[32] in O[sterode; Ostroda].[33] No excuses."

"What's wrong? What's going on? Besides, I really and truly don't have the time.... What actually goes on in your heads? Who is supposed to take over the responsibilities here, if..." but there was no point in talking any further; the other end had already hung up. The guys there are experienced and don't get caught in any conversations.

There was already a slight sense of foreboding because every once in a while something different would leak out — about the enemy's victories or the methodical withdrawal of the troops, about the sinking morale, about the overhasty construction of trenches and anti-tank ditches far behind the fronts — quite a lot of what reached us were damned unpleasant things. Now, when all hands on the farm were overwhelmed with work, now was when I should have been left in peace, without trouble, without messing around. The next eight weeks should have been peace and quiet, but instead and immediately, it was off to the front.[34]

It was useless. I had to attend, and the next day my rage grew even greater when all of my efforts to avoid the combat order failed. "To the surveillance of entrenchment work in Zone X." "*Der totale Krieg*,"[35] thus named and proclaimed by Goebbels,[36] had become reality — without regard for anyone, without regard for casualties.

---

32. *Kreis Chef* or *Kreis* boss (not to be confused with the *Kreis* leader, which was a higher level).

33. Thiel often refers to towns and camps by first letter only. This one is probably Osterode, a decent sized city a small distance from Allenstein. I have emended the rest of the German name of the town or camp to which he refers insofar as I am able to determine it, followed by the Polish name the first time the reference appears. See a full discussion of this practice of Thiel's in Appendix B, "Thiel's Sojourn," and for a comprehensive list of the placenames appearing in the memoir, see Appendix C, "Placenames," on pp. 171–174. Also, see the maps on pages 24, 42, 43, 93 and 107.

34. At this point, Thiel has been drafted into a labor and construction force activated under the *Volksaufgebot* (The People's Levy), a conscription that Berlin created to help regular troops build fortifications in East Prussia.

35. Total war.

36. Joseph Paul Goebbels, the Nazi propaganda minister.

II

Total War

We were placed in an entirely new situation. All prior engagements had to be discarded, and we still did not know how long we would be away. In a few hours I completed the necessary household tasks and took care of all necessary arrangements with banks, businessmen, and the two remaining workers who were assuming responsibility for the farm. The car gave its all one more time. Luckily, my wife and the children were accustomed to the tempo by now, and to all the unusual measures; they were no longer surprised by anything. The old hunting backpack held the essentials, equipped as if going for a hunt, but in place of the rifle or the shotgun was the reliable Mauser pistol, and strapped alongside was a sufficient amount of ammunition.

So I showed up on time at the train station in O[sterode]., and was designated co-leader of the departing transport, which consisted of about 1200 men. Fortunately, cleverness helped me to avoid taking on that position; I had no desire to assume responsibility over this motley crew of men, thrown together haphazardly, draped with various guns and firearms, which in many cases the men hardly knew how to use. Because of expected partisan attacks, we had been ordered to bring weapons....

A tremendously long D train[37] stood ready, and then off it went, curving towards an unknown destination.

The passing of that journey was almost as varied and colorful as the rabble of men around me. We knew why this campaign had

---

37. Short for *Durchgangszug*, meaning "through-train."

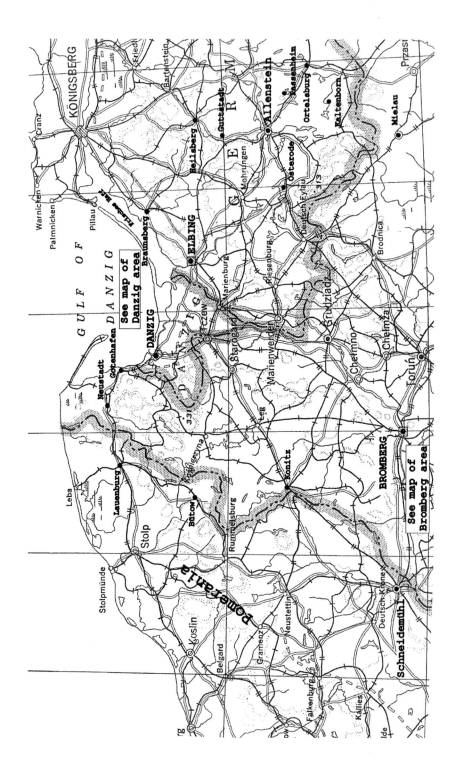

The Danzig area, where Thiel spent his last weeks of combat. He was captured
by Soviet soldiers between Gotenhafen and Danzig on March 28, 1945, the day
Gotenhafen fell to the Red Army. From a map of wartime Poland prepared by the
United States Army Map Service for the Army Chief of Staff (1943).

been launched, but where we were going was unclear. The further
we rolled eastwards, the deeper sank the barometer of our feelings,
especially since food and alcohol were running out. The stops on
empty stretches of track grew longer, the visits by the enemy recon-
naissance planes came more frequently, the taunts of the retreating
soldiers were clearer, and the rumbling artillery fire came nearer and

Opposite: Map showing the region of Thiel's sojourn — through portions of East
Prussia, the Polish Corridor, the Free City of Danzig, and Eastern Germany.
Thiel's participation in the battle of the Eastern Front and his years of imprison-
ment took him throughout this area. Significant locations in that sojourn are
highlighted. From a map of wartime Poland prepared by the United States Army
Map Service for the Army Chief of Staff (1943).

grew heavier, hour by hour. The horizon shone blood red in the night — the front was approaching.

One by one, and in groups, people made themselves scarce and disappeared. The transport leadership had long since lost track of the number of men. The commanders were seized by fear, unnerved as they walked through the train-cars in search of men with some composure and influence, hoping for support in their struggle against the frenetic, weak souls, and the defeatists. My bitterness was severe and hardly unjustified, and to my pleasant satisfaction, I wasn't alone in voicing my opposition against the splendidly uniformed leaders. Here, for the first time, one encountered a blunt and open stand against a Party and a regime that had been hated for years. To the critical observer, it became exceedingly clear how deep and insurmountable the abyss had become that separated the people from their leaders.

"We have no desire to let ourselves be slaughtered like cattle by you big shots. I'll take part, even with relish, but I'm not going to let you, you damned golden pheasant (the higher Party uniform-wearers were usually called this)[38] out of my eyes again. You'll go up to the front before me."

"I've left my bones in '14-'18,[39] at Verdun.[40] As of now, two of my sons have fallen. They[41] should make their own mess — I won't help them anymore."

"Ah, be fair! Everything's not so bad.... Ivan never enters the province, the soldier stands like iron, the new weapons are supposed to be marvels — you will see. One day he'll go back behind the Urals and everything will be just fine."

"Everything is possible if only the damned Party would disappear."

"I have heard from a dependable source that we're standing on

---

38. The term *Goldfasan* (golden pheasant) was often used to refer to Nazi party leaders. Their uniforms were brown and red, which resembled the colors of a male pheasant, but the term was also meant to draw attention to their cloying self-importance, their greed, and their common bent towards ostentatious possessions, particularly in their uniforms.

39. 1914–1918, i.e. World War I.

40. One of the costliest battles in World War I.

41. Referring to the party leaders, the *Goldfasanen* (golden pheasants).

the brink of a military dictatorship. Hitler and Göring will remain in name only; the power will lie in the hands of the generals."

Such were the conversations and opinions that you heard wherever you listened.

Rrroom, rrrroooms — and then this unpleasant sound comes a few times more, but it is already getting weaker.

"What's wrong?"

"Are we already at Ivan's?"

"Pipes and smokes out — no lighters!"

"Down on the floor!"

Tak tak tak ... again becoming weaker. A short burst of machine-gun fire. A few hits further up in the front of the car. The whole thing was just a short visit by some pilot.

The train stops soon; no one gets out. Everyone listens tensely to the motor sounds outside in the night. A few more growls from the low flying machines — it would have been nice to creep under the grass, just peeking out, so as not to miss the impressive spectacle above. But there is no more firing.

I stand outside for a long time and follow the operation tensely, but at the sound of the machines, I can only make out our own equipment and a few pieces of paper fluttering in the air nearby. I dart back into the car with a few of these slips, and under a blanket with a flashlight I read: "Kill Hitler. Then there will be Peace and Freedom and Bread. Your fronts are destroyed. Your army reports are lies. Only we tell you the truth. Come and join us in masses. We are expecting you. All further resistance is pointless, etc." No one was impressed by such clumsy propaganda. Everyone knew about the rain of paper from above, and the slips always proved useful when you had to use the toilet.

Neither the old hands who had stood at the front from '14-'18, nor the many others who had come from central and western German cities were by any means unfamiliar with the "steel blessings" from above. Nevertheless, most of the men in the transport began to grow nervous and more and more subdued, even though there was little damage and no one had been hurt. Near me was a small crowd of men whom I knew from my region, and they became practically insufferable with their repeated demands to be taken back home.

Strangely enough (and much to my dismay) I was soon regarded as a leader of sorts, looked upon for advice and possible courses of action.

At the next stop everyone had to get out, and we lined up according to car, in rows of four. We couldn't use any flashlights or matches. We were ordered to be absolutely silent. Beneath the soles of our feet were railroad ties and crushed stone, and, as we realized later, on the next line there stood a freight train filled with ammunition. Where were we?

An unfamiliar voice asks us who we are, where we come from, and what we're supposed to be doing — I find myself across from a soldier who is on duty here, and I find out where we are. I am also told that we should be very careful with lights, etc. The bombers visited here just as regularly as the partisans did. While we are still talking quietly, my name is called, accompanied by an order to attend a meeting up front immediately. The group doesn't want me to leave, but I make clear to them that I am only curious, and promise to be back as soon as possible. The soldier leads me behind him down the other side of his cars, where we can walk faster. He is just as curious as I am to find out what the orders are.

He's preoccupied with his train full of ammunition; he fears that its proximity to such a large number of unknown people could prove dangerous. We are stopped several times by guards — my soldier is an officer and the leader of the transport, and so he succeeds in sneaking me to the ward building where my command has already received orders from some SS officers.

Apparently they had already picked me for something, for when I arrive I'm immediately told "As long as you don't receive other orders, take these men to the town of D. on the shortest route possible. Here's the map — you can make a sketch for yourself. Don't worry about any special security measures because there isn't anyone in the area. There are ration stations here and here, and the distance should be about forty kilometers. You should be marching by the crack of dawn. That's all."

While he is talking, I am trying quickly to think something up. I really have no desire to accept the mission and take responsibility over such a huge number of men. I told them that there were many other accomplished soldiers and officers available, all of whom had more experience and ability than I did. The rest of the men would certainly trust a man in uniform more than they would trust me (by saying this I was partly taunting the golden pheasants who were there). I have close to no military experience, and no leadership qualities at all, and so on.... Again I was lucky; two others were chosen instead. Then the circle broke up quickly and the SS roared away, rumbling into the night with their all-terrain vehicles. They had promised earlier to take care of the food-ration distribution as quickly as possible, but nothing ever came of their promise.

A small group of Party members remained, and they stood there shaking from fear, consoling and comforting one another. The SS had, in fact, had the courtesy to inform us that the partisans and the Ivans were especially after those who wore brown uniforms,[42] so everyone who had one should try to get rid of it as soon as possible.

My companion grins broadly as he pulls me from this interesting group. "You got yourself out of that one very nicely," he said. "But that only worked because the SS were forced to deal with you as a civilian. In the future you should be more careful. We're in a war-zone here — minesweepers are always needed ahead — and the dark minds have all the power."

At his car I say goodbye, wishing him good luck. "Wait a second," he says. "I have something for you here." He climbs into his car and appears again with a canteen, filled with hot tea and rum. A more-than-welcome refreshment, it draws a little more life into my stiffening body.

Then the train station is emptied, and we stumble a few hundred meters into the dark countryside. We still have time to rest and wait for day, setting up camp between trees and shrubs and a labyrinth of deep, dry trenches. Under a thick bush I feel dry ground. My backpack becomes the pillow; my blanket is pulled up over my ears. The fearful voices and familiar questions no longer draw my attention.

Suddenly I am awakened by a shot, which certainly came from

42. Uniform of the Nazi Party, especially the SA, not of the *Wehrmacht*. SA is an abbreviation for *Sturmabteilung*, commonly known as Storm Troopers, a paramilitary unit of the Nazi Party.

a hunting gun. A wild chaos of yells and several further blasts wake me completely. With my pistol in hand, I remain lying and calmly await the unknown enemy. And then another wild chaos of swearing, running, stumbling men — and in the half-light, no one can tell where he is going. Everywhere someone is fighting, bellowing, or running for his life.

Would the partisans really have risked an attack on the camp? If yes, then, calmly, I'll let them come nearer. Eight rounds are ready, and I have the second magazine loaded and at hand. But I can't make out any Russian or Polish words. Perhaps they've already cleared out. I call out several of my companion's names, but receive no answer. Their camping spots are still recognizable, however, for I can see the pieces from their baggage scattered about. But the heroes themselves have disappeared.

The gunfire has stopped. The men call out names and locations, and I can hear them respond to each other. "What is wrong?" They ask me over and over again, and since I have been smoking for some time now, soon more of the calming sticks glow among the men in the circle. They all try hard to appear as if they are just waking up, as if nothing at all has shaken them.

Even many months after we left, we still talked and laughed about that hour near the small fortress of O. Many of those involved didn't enjoy remembering how they had scraped their heads and legs in a wild flight through roots and trees, or remembering how one or another of them found himself unhurt but with only one shoe or boot, the other never to be found. The result was a small number of fractures and sprains, but luckily no one was killed.

A Lithuanian laborer had gotten hungry and began to look through a large farmer's box in search of something edible; he was discovered and throttled. His groans woke up someone nearby who had a rifle and was probably dreaming especially vivid dreams about partisans. This man quickly fired off an alarm that brought the whole sleeping camp to its legs and made everyone frantic. Those who still wore brown uniforms had taken the whole incident very badly — the last fragments they had of composure went straight to hell, and, as we found out later, they had climbed as quickly as possible into an empty, returning train and disappeared.

The march to D. lasted almost three days because on the way we frequently received other orders. The older men had a hard time dealing with the heat, and the streets were filled to the brim with tanks and vehicles of every sort, so our platoon became more and more torn apart. Hunger, and even more significantly, thirst, depressed the general atmosphere and morale; all the fountains and pumps were contaminated or disconnected. Ration stations were everywhere, yet we couldn't use them because we didn't have the special permission required. So in small, splintered columns the transport dragged itself along the streets without any organized leadership.

A group of nearly 140 men stubbornly regards me as their leader,[43] and we keep the lead until reaching D. Most of us are sore by the time we come to the Russian-Polish town; we are hungry, exhausted, and ill-tempered. I report our arrival to the town's commanding officer. He receives me rudely, as if we are an unexpected addition to his problems, and he'd rather we were in hell. Neither food nor lodging awaits us; in fact, they don't have any use for us at all. I begin to understand that we are completely superfluous, that the organization has failed entirely.

The area was already occupied by the O.T.[44] (*Organization Todt*, i.e. *Autobahn*, *Westwall*, *Atlantikwall*, and *Ostwall*), a military labor organization, and so we were only a burden. My rage had grown greater than my disappointment, but what could one do? The destination had been reached, and we thought it pointless to look for work, while at home more than enough already awaited us. So there was nothing to do but return westward in the direction of home, though before we did anything, we had to eat and rest.

Eventually I got permission from the local commanders to use two of the field kitchens,[45] and they let me borrow some coffee and

---

43. Thiel uses the German *Leithammel* here, which literally translates as "bellwether," though I doubt he intends the negative connotation often associated with the term's figurative use.

44. *Organization Todt*: The major Germany construction organization under the Third Reich founded by the engineer and senior Nazi party member, Dr. Fritz Todt. He directed the building of Germany's *Autobahn* and wide-spread military installations and fortifications, including a number of defensive "walls," such as those mentioned here by Thiel. Albert Speer controlled the organization after Todt's death in 1942.

45. Thiel uses the military slang for field kitchen: *Gulaschkanonen*, meaning, literally, "goulash cannon."

potatoes, a little bit of meat, and some cans of lard as well. The sharpest-witted men of the group had come with me, and they quickly understood what to do. So as I distracted the camp leader and told him stories, they stole additional supplies. After a little while, we were finally able to stuff ourselves again.

We found some empty rooms as well, so I had the men line up, took a head count, and reported the number to the military police where I had been ordered to go. Once again they chose me as the leader, and quickly provided me with a newly issued identification card. I didn't make any objections this time — though, of course, it wasn't because of the fine cognac that these sympathetic, weather-beaten fellows offered me in huge quantities.

But then they didn't let us leave. They made us a special division with our own command and our own administration. I constructed a work-schedule that was as reasonable as possible. I was given access to three adjacent farms to use for lodging, and I had permission to do with them as I saw fit. A businessman became the quartermaster sergeant, two butchers became the kitchen cooks, two school teachers kept the roll of names, a few older men were quartermasters, and others were group-leaders and foremen, etc.

I tried my best to be wherever something smelled of money, food, alcohol, or some type of tobacco product. At the bottom of it all the men just wanted to live, and to my satisfaction they were happy with their leader.

With the help of the local people — and without any regard for the crops or the woods — we built trenches, anti-tank defense holes, and other deep and wide anti-tank ditches. We cut firing lanes through the forests as well — anything and everything that was necessary to stop and defeat possible attackers. The work was not always easy; when we dug holes in the meadows or the low-lying areas, they quickly filled up with water after just a few shovels-full.

Wounded and convalescing experienced soldiers of all ranks were sent to help us with the technical instructions. Interactions with them were enjoyable; they brought me hours and hours of unforgettable conversation and relaxation that I never had at home. The work tempo was not too bad either. We never had to push ourselves or exaggerate what we had done. If ever a PKW (*Personenkraftwagen*)[46] happened to appear with some brown-shirted commanding officer who wanted to see the progress we had made, or just hear something new, then we immediately changed the topic of conversation and resumed our work. A friendly relationship with these commanders was, and remained, an impossibility, even when they made efforts in that direction.

Trouble was brewing throughout the ranks of the *Wehrmacht*. The men began to realize the absurdity and pointlessness of the battle. The younger boys were fed up too, and now they only hoped for a miracle, or a quick end. Here at the front, the hatred for the Party (and its bigwig officials) was perhaps more pervasive, and the same sentiments were widely shared by all ranks of men — from the lowest-ranked soldier to officers on the general staff. One saying known by everyone was: "Hitler must be eliminated, or else it is only a matter of time before everything goes to the dogs."

But unfortunately, we soldiers were not in a position to do anything. We could only do what we were commanded to do, and beyond that, we didn't have the slightest bit of influence. And unless the generals order us differently, we can't just let Ivan waltz in here either, as if he were a "guest," and introduce him to our wives....

Day and night our thoughts revolved around these issues, and in the evenings we were able to meet in the M.P.'s[47] quarters and talk. It was a small, select, group of men, gathering to speak frankly about those things that went through our minds, and we were able to do so with the help of Ukrainian *Hiwis* (helpers) and others who had reasons to hide from the Russians — together they formed a thick ring around the area, and guarded it both dependably and effectively.

The military brought these fellows here with their wives and kids. They stuck them into black uniforms, furnished them with plenty of weapons, and allowed them to live as they wanted. So they had at their disposal a troop of completely faithful, ruthless, scouts, who were especially adept at searching out and fighting guerilla groups in the vicinity.

---

46. A private motorcar.
47. The word here is *Feldgendarmerie*, an earlier term for military police.

You had to be familiar with the attitude and convictions of these old battle-hardened *gendarmes* to believe how these black devils responded to the faintest sign, and silently and dependably took action regardless of whom they had to fight or what it had to do with. Beginning in Caucasia, this excellent troop had shared everything with one another, from joy to sorrow, and the disappearance of many a parasite or Party big-shot can be credited to them. In fact, never again would I experience a hardened, unconditional unity such as theirs.

And if one time or another I became curious, one of them full of strong alcohol might for a moment let himself go, and tell me how one of his comrades had been discovered — with a swastika cut in his stomach and chest, his fingers nailed individually to a board, along with his toes, the tongue cut out — he must have lived for a few more hours. Another was bound to a tree with barbed wire; at his feet there had been a fire. Another had been made to choke on his own genitals, etc. To the regularly half drunk "defenders of right and order," the term humanity no longer had any meaning.

One night, someone stole my good old Mauser pistol. I wanted, and needed, to find a replacement, and I could only hope to get one at the M.P. station. The captain didn't think long before he guaranteed its recovery within the course of the day. He told me, however, that I should speak with Wassyl about reward money, and Wassyl (hetman[48] of the black guard) was suddenly in the picture, standing before us. He and some of his men knew the Mauser, and everyone's eyes lit up at the high reward offer. So the whole company took off on the way to my farm.[49] Some of them blocked off everything in a wide radius while the others swarmed like rats through the rooms and searched. We waited nearby and calmly smoked our cigars, discussing who we thought might have been the culprit. "I'll get you the weapon no matter what!" someone said, "And then I'll bring the thief back here and we'll finish him off! We're at the front now; I will judge the stealing of weapons according to our laws here!"

48. A hetman is a headman, or leader.
49. i.e., where Thiel was encamped.

I began to get anxious and cursed what I had done. By no means would I allow a human life to be taken for this. I managed to get a half promise that they wouldn't search for the thief. The pistol was found buried in hay in a barn outside the living quarters. The thief, doubtless a familiar and disreputable character, spent days fearing for his life.

After nearly three weeks, the operation seemed, to us at least, to have come to an end. Packed into a LKW,[50] we rode to the next big train station. We arrived at home in the middle of the harvest, rich with new impressions.

A number of months filled with difficult work followed, and they proved to be the last of their kind. Today, only memories remain of the house, of the garden and the family — of home. In November there was another fourteen-day course in M[ielau; Mława]., Poland, to train instructors of anti-tank defense. The instructors who were there were, in part, highly decorated and successful soldiers and specialists in the field. The days there were interesting and peaceful, and a true period of rest for me. In the meantime, not only did the bombs explode steadily throughout the poor shattered cities, but also the fronts were moved back daily "for strategic reasons." We watched as the collapse grew more complete, and yet we still didn't want to believe that the Russians would cross the German border. Sending your families westward was forbidden, and it would have been wrong and irresponsible to send them in the direction of the bombs; anyway, this also would have meant giving up your house and your farm.

Many years later I thought about that time, and came to the same conclusion. We handled it correctly.[51] Every day heavier and heavier assaults come down on Berlin or Kassel, and at any particular hour it was always uncertain whether your relatives were still alive. To make any type of telephone contact was only possible at the military offices, and only if a good friend was sitting there when you came.

50. *Lastkraftwagen*, a shipping truck.
51. Thiel must mean here that they handled it correctly by remaining at home as long as possible.

In the first days of January 1945 I received another draft order. I immediately tried to enroll with the active troops, but was unsuccessful, and my time was measured — I had to go with my orders.

The *Volkssturm* was put into action. For this last ditch effort, the leaders rounded up everyone who was still capable of standing and moving on his own two feet without someone else's help. Germany's last contingent of men now entered the war.

A small circle of high officers stationed in the area willingly agreed to arrange an evacuation of my family if necessary. For a few weeks before I left, they were frequent and welcome visitors at my home, and we often went hunting together. Thanks to good connections in the state forest, where I'd been allowed to shoot for some time now, I was able to find a number of good goats, some stags and sows for these men. One of the men was General N., the commander of an army group, and the others were members of his closest staff. They were all excellent people, and I haven't heard anything about them since. But they kept their word, and in the final hours they carried my wife and children to safety.

In any case, the atmosphere at my departure was not the best. You didn't have to be clairvoyant to realize that the clock had now struck twelve, and it was the moment of truth. So to the two people who remained, I could only suggest that they take care of my family, and give them hints about fleeing, if that became necessary. It would have been pointless to put things in order or make plans. Everything paled next to the knowledge that darker events were coming.

Again my backpack was as light as possible. Only the old Mauser pistol received an especially careful inspection. Then one last visit to the peacefully sleeping children, and off I went.

Dear God. What a motley gang of randomly chosen men! Was this Hitler's last measure of retaliation? The special weapon that was supposed to give the battle that long awaited turn in our favor? Men from all professions had appeared, from all classes of society, aging anywhere from seventeen to seventy. They were hunchbacks, cripples, some almost blind, and they were in any number of moods: though none in a mood to fight. And this crowd of men was supposed to be trained and deployed as quickly as possible —

As far as it was necessary (or as far as they were available), uniforms with a civilian cut were supplied from army supply stores, but it wasn't until later that everyone wore the nationality insignia on his cap. A certain number of stars differentiated the ordinary man from his superiors and showed the rank of the wearer. Everyone who hadn't brought his own weapon got an Italian or Czech military rifle (some of them without straps) and a cartridge pouch with fifty rounds. A robber baron would have been quite delighted by our varied and colorful troops.

We were a completely new, separately deployed unit. We did, of course, have to stay in contact with the other regular units, but for the most part we acted independently. This system didn't work, and as it later turned out, it cost us heavy, unnecessary casualties.

We received accommodations in the Masurian town of K[altenborn; Zimnawoda]., not far from the well-known military training area A. Some of the general staff were also in K[altenborn]. to carry out the training and deployment of the division. Food and lodging were good, and because I hardly encountered any acquaintances here, it was easy to lag behind undisturbed, carefully checking things over and forming impressions. I was essentially able to ignore a number of questions about some or another particular training or instruction.

Anyway, I'd had it up to here with the whole lot of them, and it was revolting to have to do a new training course. I hoped that through some favorable circumstance I might receive a suitable, cushy job, where I would be somewhat independent and, most importantly, didn't have to carry too much responsibility. A job in a supply area (PX), driving a vehicle, or something similar would work well. When my company commander was looking for someone who knew about the telephone and writing materials....

"Yes, here I am."

"Well come along," he said. I should have kept my mouth shut as I had earlier, because after a short cross-examination the otherwise very nice but inexperienced man had appointed me "*Spiess*."[52] In the army, the "*Spiess*" is the mother of the company. He is more

52. Slang, roughly translated as "top sergeant."

important to the men than the commander is, and is also generally better respected. In our organization, we tried to follow the army as exactly as possible.

One day, to my frustration and to the joy of the commander, I was sitting down in the midst of our work when the division leader stopped his car and made us report to him. Still, it was a pleasant surprise for both of us, for we had known each other from before. We had been split up for a few years, but had spent some very good times together.

"Why don't you have your own company?" he asked me. "You're not going to avoid anything around here. Anyway, I have a more suitable job for you for right now. Come along immediately."

So then I became the town commander for K[altenborn]. and commander of the division's area, which included the school-house, the teachers' quarters, and the local offices. For day and night I worked like a bee in a hive — I always had to be in close contact with the corresponding offices of the active troops in the vicinity. It was responsibility, just as I didn't want, and by the ton. I got very little sleep, the very best of the food, and a constant flow of curious visitors who wanted to hear straight from the horse's mouth how things actually were. By night the over-tired leaders played cards with alcohol and the radio nearby in anxious expectation of the newest reports. Every now and then, reports made it through, informing us of the actual status of shifting troops at the fronts.

The alert level — 2 during the day and 1 at night — was never lifted. That, along with the generally bad conditions, was a great strain on your nerves. For the time being, we still lacked the iron calm that characterized those hard-nosed, experienced men who had spent long stretches at the front.

And then one day we finished our training, were declared prepared for battle, and put to a march. Before we went, I dressed myself as splendidly as possible. I could do this because, along with the secret files and the telephones, I was the last one to leave the town, and the LKW was waiting there with almost everything a soldier desired. The drivers were stunned by my calm as I took the goods from the truck, dressing those friends of mine who were still along, wrapping them in the most beautiful and newest camouflage furs, searching out clothes and blankets and pieces of uniforms and the best driving jackets — and then distributing them all among the men as if we were starting some calm and comfortable journey home.

Since we were heading closer to the front, I was unable to take along the few remaining civilians in our area, who must have watched our departure with mixed feelings. Now our destination was G[uttstadt; Dobre Milasto]., and even though the distance was hardly eighty kilometers, it took two days of travel and a series of forced stops before we groped our way into the town. On the way, the numerous patches of woods proved to be fortunate. There, in peace, we could size up our bodies and check over our vehicles.

The "*Jabos*,"[53] the low-flying fighter pilots, watched the streets like hawks twenty-four hours a day, reminding us of gymnastic exercises long since forgotten. Even though they flew badly, the group was generally unpleasant, for we had to assume that they would make some lucky strikes — sufficiently graphic proof could be found in the ditches on the side of the road.

The district town of O[rtelsburg; Szccytn]., which was familiar to me, received its first heavy air-raid as we passed. There were several fires; for the most part the locals were either in their cellars or in the entranceways of their homes. Several nearby strikes forced us to stop and look for cover. Then, later, we watched for the opportunity to meet each other and arrange a time to leave.

Two long trains were at the train station, filled with refugees and ready to depart. The poor passengers surveyed the effects of the air-raids, considering what would probably be left of their town if the planes returned. "Let's just go, away from here and these bare railroad tracks, where we're defenseless against the falling bombs. Enough of this tiresome waiting." "Will we finally be rolling soon?" "Will we make it beyond the Vistula?" "Where are the Russians?" "Is it that you really can't, or that you aren't allowed to tell us anything?" "Why don't you give us some kind of assurances?" "Is it true that the Russians have committed war-atrocities?" — I knew a few of the people who were leaving their homes asking these questions. I

---

53. i.e. *Jagdbomber*, a fighter-bomber — here, obviously, Soviet planes.

escaped them as quickly as possible. They weren't able to bring anything along, except food and the most necessary clothes.

I tried to arrange a telephone conversation with my family, but all my attempts were in vain. I was only twenty-two kilometers away as the crow flies, but the telephone lines were destroyed, and I couldn't even find the military command where I had a few friends. I was conflicted — should I take advantage of the opportunity — should I just get out of my uniform and go home to my wife and children? On the one hand, I saw the whole situation as complete and utter madness. But on the other hand, there was the danger I wouldn't find anyone at home anyway, and then desertion would be pointless.

No, and once more — no. I had my duties here, and you can't just leave your comrades in the lurch. We had a score to settle with Ivan.

We arrived at our destination of G[uttstadt]., and found it overcrowded with various different divisions of corps, yet there wasn't a single person from our group. Because I was known here, we received lodging right away and rested well, having become our own small command (in O[rtelsburg]. three men could make up their own command). I parked the LKW in a deserted corner where it was well camouflaged.

We had more than enough to eat, but unfortunately I wasn't allowed any peace. The head of the local civilian offices, the local government leader, and the mayor were soon all regular guests, so my quarters quickly became *the* office where everyone came to meet. This included farmers, refugees, and more than anything else the quartermasters. They happily and willingly obeyed my orders because in contrast to the normal bureaucracy they had known, I settled everything immediately and verbally. The other "administrative machinery" was nothing more than a group of rigid, old farmers whom I knew well. They had lost all connection with any higher office, but yet continued, even given the circumstances, to insist stubbornly on orders and regulations that had lost all of their legitimacy.

The people here were also simply inept. After all of their experiences, they had learned only to be anxious about whether or not they had done something wrong, and how to avoid undertaking any responsibility. I still had the men's trust from before, so for several days and nights I became the center of G[uttstadt].; I was the most frequently searched for and questioned civilian steward in town. One day my division commander discovered me so busy that he was more than a little surprised, especially since on the way someone had informed him of my death. The reunion was richly celebrated, and the civilian incident was forgotten for good.[54]

We studied the maps and discussed plans for the deployment of troops. The situation had changed since last I heard. It seemed as if the fronts had come to a standstill, with serious fighting on both sides. The *Volkssturm* was supposed to be sent in as support for the active troops, to reinforce them in the especially vulnerable places, and then also to be deployed wherever necessary.

With the approval of the active troops,[55] we are committed to a certain *Abschnitt*.[56] The dispatch rider was ready with the orders for the units scattered about the area. We could finally start in the direction of the front.

It became my task to take care of the ammunition supply and establish a depot, using a number of trucks and several teams of commandeered horse-carts. While we were still planning, the *Kreisleiter*[57] (the highest political spokesman and the most powerful politician of the district) appeared and requested help in evacuating some people from towns next to the front. I left right away.

In O. I received some reinforcement in the form of further trucks and escorts. The column groped its way towards the front, through blocked up towns and heavily darkened streets. On the way we collected people who had decided to wait things out and remain until the last possible minute. In the apartment buildings we found those who were too old or too weak to leave by themselves, or who

54. It seems that he is referring to the incident when the commander found him sitting on the job.
55. The *Wehrmacht*.
56. *Abschnitt*, in this context, could mean "regiment." But more likely Thiel is referring to an administrative "sector" of the SS or SD (*Sicherheitsdienst*, the security service of the SS).
57. *Kreisleiter*, i.e., the *Kreis* leader. The *Kreis* was one of the Nazis' administrative sectors, smaller than a *Gau*.

had missed the connection for the main train, or who just simply didn't want to leave.

As far as we had space, we crammed the people into the vehicles, allowing them the least baggage possible, and took them back to a reception station. During the trip our passengers made great demands of the drivers, and of the "human beings" in us. The former were completely exhausted and had to fight with darkness and innumerable other obstacles. As for the rest of us, we were just as exhausted by our responsibility for the passengers. But even harder was dealing with the frequent, merciless decisions we had to make — to leave the eighty-year old man, or, if necessary, to leave the whole family.

There's not enough time or room to take everyone to safety. The Russians could be here at any minute; we can't form anything resembling a clear picture from the contradictory statements of our soldiers. In any case, only this much can be certain — we are snatching the last civilians from the grasp of the Russians.

The enormous hatred for the criminal, irresponsible propaganda and for the completely failing organization rises through us rapidly. These poor men could have been taken back comfortably, if someone had only come a few weeks earlier, or even a few days. But instead, that pile of rabble had been carrying on about well-established fronts, successful counterattacks, "everyone has to remain at home," "if it became necessary, they would tell people to flee," and so on.

It was a heavy strain on the nerves to have to watch the women and children throwing themselves over their weak or older, bed-ridden relatives as they said good-bye. Likewise to see women lie down in front of the overfilled trucks, holding their infants and children, trying to force us to take some other relative who still remained. Or to see a mother finally brought along with her two smallest children, as she realizes that in the commotion her third has been pushed aside and lost. Another throws someone else's bag from the truck, so that there is room for him. And for the life of me, I could no longer close the back of the truck, for the desperate faces don't want to give up their last chance to get on, not for any price. The poor people are clinging to me like leeches, and the promises to come again don't help at all. My men have to rescue me with force

..., and so on we went several more times, though in other directions on similarly dangerous, unpleasant and exhausting runs to the front.

Then I am forced to give up that job, and I must switch immediately to the ammunitions depot. Real coffee and alcohol are delivered in large quantities and keep us going. We travel through the next two days and nights, even when a burst of gunfire from a Mpi (*Maschinenpistole*)[58] attacks us in a patch of forest. It's disconcerting in a way that other things haven't been, but we don't let it stop us. We know now that a scouting party has advanced to our position and grown bold.

At the next base we write up a short report about the "raid," and then continue marching. In the school at the town of S., I set up a mini-camp. It lies alone in the midst of an extensive forest and is supposed to serve as an important base. A group of regular army engineers is also there. They are supposed to establish mine fields at the bridges, in the forest, and at other strategic points. One day after an excellent meal in his quarters, the friendly captain puts me gently but firmly in a fur jacket and prescribes that I have at least one night of complete rest.

After a few hours the darkness has closed in, and then some soldier rolls me brusquely off the couch. Complete confusion overwhelms the house. By the glow of flashlights, people search for all kinds of things — steel helmets and gasmasks clatter on belts; handgrenades and ammunition belts are adjusted. Even in my half-sleep I see it immediately — we're in combat. It's probably still far away, but a few strikes and the typical sound of mortar fire quickly chase away any trace of fatigue.

The first fire that flares up at a neighboring farm makes my flashlight unnecessary. I leave my fur coat behind, hanging only a few "pineapples"[59] on my belt. One last snack from the opened cans — a bar of chocolate goes in my bag — cigarettes. I take a generous swallow from the bottle of cognac, and then I look for my men. It's futile. I begin to realize that they must have awakened

---

58. A submachine gun.

59. A common slang term for hand grenades. The actual German slang is *Eier*, meaning "eggs."

earlier, climbed into the trucks as quickly as possible, and made a run for it.

The fire has expanded, and now it lights up the whole nearby village. It looks as if it's completely deserted, except for a soldier who is running towards me and escaping. He tells me where the commanding officer is, and I discover that he's actually at his command post. He's astonished by my appearance, and visibly happy to have added a "man" to his tiny forces. His soldiers were deployed in forest bunkers throughout the area of S.; his headquarters only had about forty men. Our chances were the worst possible you could imagine. Apparently we were completely surrounded. Yet because of the dense patches of forest where the enemy could quickly deploy its troops, the last dispatch riders could not say anything definite about our status. In a short time, Ivan learned how to provide lighting: with mortars and fire-trails following the shells. It was a perfectly marvelous, unforgettable picture — the number of blazes multiplied, and in so doing they illuminated the whole town, along with the edge of the woods lying behind, and about one and half kilometers of snow-covered strips of land. It was as light as if it were day.

Just as soon as a head ventured over the brink of a trench, rifle bullets whizzed by, followed by a machine-gun burst of fire, and shortly thereafter you would hear the unwelcome explosion from a mortar.

Then we hear the whistling. Our seasoned veterans grab their steel helmets, conduct a customary scan of their belts, and quickly nod to one another. They know that at the third whistle the Russians will attack. And sure enough a chanting, howling mass erupts from the edge of the forest and surges towards us. It looks as if a herd of cattle is being driven into a corral by several loudly roaring cattle-drivers.

When they're a hundred meters away, the commanding officer gives the order to fire. The LMG (*Leichtes Masch[inen]. Gewehr*)[60] has perfect aim, and the effects are what you would expect. The first wave has been repulsed. Elsewhere near us it's the same picture.

60. A light machine gun.

Then we are "softened up" with mortar fire. There are the first dead. The wounded are looked after quickly, but they can't be removed.

We're only a handful of men now. We know that the next wave won't be stopped, that no reinforcements are on the way, that a counterattack would be suicide, and that getting away is impossible. This time at the third whistle two crowds take off from the edge of the woods. They are under fire even before they're a hundred meters away, but we can't stop them. I have both of my last ammunition belts ready. Their course changes. Our gunner picks his shots carefully. The commanding officer diligently stacks up the hand grenades, but can't dig up any extra magazines for his submachine gun. I have already gotten the four available *Panzerfäuste*[61] ready. They are lying next to another pair of my rifles, with tons of ammunition.

And then everything happened like it does in the movies. No one thought of taking cover anymore. Everyone fired as fast and as often as possible — and always into the midst of that slowly onward rolling, heavily drunken, howling heap of men. The LMG, our main weapon, grew silent. The belts of ammunition are used up. The throng is coming even faster now. We can still use the rifles. One after another I shoot them until they're empty. The distance is still too great to use the Mauser, but a *Panzerfaust* will serve me well. Its effects are baffling, aimed right into the center of the crowd. The commanding officer shoots off the second one. I shoot the third. The area becomes free of enemies. The racket momentarily sobered the crowd of drunken attackers and gave the survivors long legs. We decide to quit and check over the other sections of trench. We hurry down the trenches with our pistols in hand, followed by the three men who are still remaining. On the strip we see wounded men helping each other, and then the dead, who no longer need help.

We leave the trenches and push through the burning town. One man points to some figures that are moving as we are — we hear Russian words and disappear as quickly as possible into the other direction. The town is occupied by Ivan. We roam about like mice in a

---

61. A *Panzerfaust* is a simple, single-use anti-tank weapon similar to the American bazooka. *Panzerfäuste* is the plural form.

trap. Time and again we find an open stretch of land, but are unable to summon the courage that would permit us to run straight into Ivan's arms without any cover — like handing ourselves over on a silver platter. But finally we have no other choice, and a miracle occurs — we make it to the forest without any problem.

We march stubbornly towards the north, remaining within shouting distance of one another. Finally we are stopped by one of our advance parties. We arrive at an estate under our control, and to a chorus of hellos and astonished faces we present ourselves to the staff as the only escapees from the surrounded area of S. — we are one engineer captain, one sergeant, one regular man, and one *Volkssturm* man. My division leader has pitched his tents there as well, and is shocked by our situation report. They hadn't thought that the Russians were so close by, and certainly not in such number and strength.

Our departure was arranged right away, but as it turned out, I decided to accept the commanding officer's offer to change my uniform and remain with him.[62] Perhaps a successful retreat would have been a better idea, but I would have been acting unfaithfully to my old "leader."

One day later another incident brought us together. He was coming along a railway embankment near my observation post, and we greeted one another with shouts. He halted and, pointing sideways, gave his men an order. As he did so, a bullet caught him through the head. One of his men beat me to getting his wallet. A Rhinelander, the commanding officer was a magnificent soldier and human being, one I came to appreciate very much in the short time I was there. And that was the way he met his end.

During the course of these days, I found several opportunities to get even with Ivan. A SMG (*Schweres Masch[inen]. Gewehr*),[63] as well as several of the tried and true *Panzerfäuste*, were always by my side and well-guarded. In critical situations, these splendid toys always gave us a moment to catch our breath, even if it was only for

---

62. At this point, Thiel's military status takes on an ambiguity as a *Volkssturm* man among army regulars. That ambiguity becomes a problem when he is captured.
63. A heavy machine gun.

a short time. There was my division captain S., a first lieutenant (he had been wounded multiple times in the old war — his profession was a schoolteacher, but he was a tough, cold, daredevil), and some other men who were just as friendly. We were inseparable. We were able to set up some bases and keep comfortable, but unfortunately, we were isolated from the main force right up to the end.

Connections could be made with some places behind the front, and orders could also make it through in that direction, but unfortunately it just didn't matter anymore. It was really hard to demand enthusiasm and courage from the men — some of whom were not even trained — when the Russians were everywhere. There was a state of panic. Because of the hopelessness, the yearning for security (and thus the desire to run away) could no longer be fought. The troops — though they could not be considered a coherent unit, for they actually consisted of several small, stationary groups, scattered throughout the area — were completely fed up. Everywhere they were, the men made a splendid showing, but then both they and we lost all ability to contact the bases behind the front. We were battle-weary throughout the ranks.

We were able to direct one of our tanks towards a strategic point, and it proved totally effective. This spicy surprise must have stayed in Ivan's memory. Then the crew got out of the "machine," and there was a muffled explosion as one of the steel walls peeled off. The young men had come here on their last drops of gas. Now they weren't hunting anything anymore.

We break away from the enemy. The destination is O[sterode?]. We creep westwards in disordered, small and larger groups, loaded up with ammunition and light weapons — raked heavily by Russian artillery (and our own as well), tanks, and anti-aircraft guns. The accompanying music of splintering trees and branches is equally unpleasant. But we have no casualties, and so we move on, and when we reach the old familiar suburban houses of O[sterode?]., we are pretty well worn out.

Russian fire is falling on the city, and well-camouflaged among the houses, a large number of tanks returns the fire. In the meantime, the enemy has advanced from another direction, and we're getting some gunfire from the flank. We are forced to take cover, and with one short sprint at a time we try to move farther individually, or in small groups.

The first lieutenant with me gets shot in the ankle, and I help him hobble into one of the small, connected houses. I look for an aid station — medical orderlies had probably been here at one time. Despite his insistence, I can't just leave him behind. In one of the neighboring, long since emptied houses I find a toboggan, as well as a pair of jars with canned sausage, bread, and butter.

In the meantime, the patient has made his own emergency dressings for the wound. We stuff ourselves until we're almost sick — I also found enough to drink. Then we set out, or, that is, I dragged him. The frail little sled frequently tipped over and threw the wounded man into the snow, but, giving the town a wide berth, we finally reached a protective patch of forest to the north. We couldn't find an aid station here either, and no medical orderlies in sight.

It grew even colder. His foot swelled up more and began to change all kinds of colors. With the help of another man, I pulled the pain-riddled lieutenant into a town that was several kilometers away. There I was finally able to find him the necessary salve. Then I made myself comfortable on a stretcher nearby, and, under his watch, I slept through the night and half a day, until he had to get on the train.

On the way back we came under artillery fire. As ordered, I took a truck back to a barrack square in the city zone, where a number of soldiers were preoccupied with zealously dragging away everything possible from a burning supply depot. Then they ran to their vehicles and disappeared. Running, quickly orienting themselves, and then grabbing the stuff — all done surprisingly fast. And it was necessary to hurry, for the smoke was getting thicker and thicker, and inside, piled up by the ton and sorted precisely, were the things that excited every soldier's heart, the things that were never issued and that we always talked about happily — simple fur-lined boots, gloves that actually matched, warm new underwear, socks, the most beautiful, light, camouflage furs, hats, undercoats, sweaters, all types of tobacco products straight from the factory, alcohol, chocolate, canned-goods, etc.

I didn't exchange my hunting boots or the old Mauser pistol, but

I stocked up with double of everything else. Sweating profusely, I dragged away jackets tied together with fur camouflage pants filled up with all those wonderful things. On the long run to the forest, about one and a half kilometers, I stumbled with my load — I was scared I would fall right into Ivan's arms, looking perfectly ridiculous.

Happily, I make it to the command station, but no one recognizes me until I speak — my appearance has changed so drastically. But all the men are electrified when the pants and sleeves are opened up and the contents are distributed among them. Never before or after did they put together a scouting party as quickly as they do now, hoping to return with more of the same plunder.

The commander gets the second camouflaged fur jacket, and the bits of nourishment in my spoils are quickly handed out, though there's still enough left over to feed my stomach through the next few days. Then the "scouting" party comes back with empty hands; it seems the shelling and the thickening smoke had become too dangerous. The artillery fire and now the heavier air-bombardments make sure that no one gets any rest. Because of the smoke, cooking and trying to get warm are hardly possible, and during the night, the cold is the worst.

There's an order to retreat in the direction of the H[eilsberger]. *Dreieck*,[64] and we must start marching immediately — movement is only permitted at night. On the streets and paths there is constant traffic of single columns or small groups, and none of them is capable of communicating with one another — all of the different corps are shoving through the chaos. Everyone is watching out for himself, pushing along at his own speed. Among them you can see some farmer who decided to flee at the very last minute, followed in the confusion by his wife, child, cow and cart.

It is here that we hear a surprising story for the first time, a

---

64. After Germany was separated from East Prussia (by the Polish Corridor) according to the Treaty of Versailles, the Reich needed to rethink its defense fortifications. In 1931, construction began on a widely dispersed fortified line around Königsberg consisting of anti-tank obstacles, machine gun bunkers and barbed wire. The line formed a triangle (*Dreieck* in German), and since the point of the triangle lay near Heilsberg, the fortifications became known as the *Heilsberger Dreieck*. Despite all the preparation, the *Heilsberger Dreieck* proved to be little trouble for the Red Army.

story we repeat later when it is confirmed by others: just as the carts have been loaded up by the farmers and they are ready to go, a Russian patrol appears. Thinking that they have breathed their last breath on earth, the poor people are frightened to death. But the Russians lend a hand. They help the farmers finish loading up their carts. They harness the horses and let the housewife give them something to eat. The farmer fetches something to drink. They are friendly and wish them a good trip — "Don't be afraid of us," they say, "But be careful now. When the second wave comes through with the commissar,[65] then it not good."

It's impossible to find any quarters that aren't overcrowded. Sleep is a great luxury. Our legs simply don't want to go any further. If you're lucky you might find a field kitchen that still has a few warm meals left — but otherwise we have to tighten our belts. For the most part, the inhabitants of the town are already gone. We are much too tired to take care of ourselves. Our retinue, two tractors with trailers and six horses-carts, can't be found, so our baggage is on the casualty list as well. Refugees from other directions tell of atrocities. The mood, already bad, is not getting better.

The animals left behind bellow in their stables with hunger and thirst, or they roam about half-frozen in the fields and in the forest. Because of the icy paths, heavy artillery, tanks, tractors of all strengths and sizes, LKW and PKW are all sliding around. Some are flipped over and abandoned by their drivers. One car is towing another. There's a lack of fuel; broken wheels; cars filled with refugees have crashed into one another; fallen, helpless animals lying on the side of the road; women and children crying; listless old men sitting in the snow; swearing military policemen who try in vain to bring some order to this chaos. The whole image is the perfect depiction of horror.

In the town of S. we decide to take a break, expecting that our baggage train with perhaps some other men will stop to take an

---

65. The political commissioner. Christel Weiss Brandenburg also recounts an incident of Russian soldiers warning German civilians about the occupation troops to follow. See *Ruined by the Reich: Memoir of an East Prussian Family, 1916–1945* (McFarland and Company, 2003), pp. 126–127. Brandenburg then describes the predicted brutal treatment by those occupying forces (see pp. 128 ff.).

inventory. Designated sentries stop everything that is wearing our colors. With our trap we manage to catch one tractor, three horse-carts, and about eighty men. My faithful shadow, D., a businessman from F., whom I had known before, is driving one of the horses. Beaming, he shows me all his baggage along with several nutritious little things he was able to obtain for the two of us on the way. He was well known here in S., and so soon we had good quarters for everyone. It had been a long time, but now we were finally able to shape our bodies back into something that resembled men. We were permitted a complete day of rest, and we slept right through it without a single order. Even the written reports that were long since due remained untouched and unnoticed.

Our platoon moved itself again, approaching the commanded destination. On the way the situation hardly changed at all — but the enemy's arm couldn't reach us. We were left unmolested, so the opinion was widely held that the Russians would dull their teeth on the strong, well fortified H[eilsberger]. *Dreieck*. And then the long awaited counterattack would follow and sweep the province clean.

The closer we came to the more distant towns, which didn't have the problems of the refugees and the *Wehrmacht*, the more they seemed to have an almost "peaceful" impression. No one in these places wanted to admit that the situation could become dangerous. Only the most anxious souls were packing their things and seriously thinking about fleeing. In the small city of R., it was impossible to buy a few small personal supplies without marks. And the man behind the store counter still clung to regulations and rules produced by a system that in our view had long since lost all authority. Here "officialdom" still thrived, as it always had.

In this town I was able to take the opportunity to visit a relative who owned a butcher's shop. It was doing well for him and was filled sky-high with good meats. With my "staff," five men whom I had rounded up, we descended upon the hospitable house and thoroughly enjoyed fresh, warm sausage in huge quantities, as well as many other tasty treats (without marks). Afterwards our stomachs were completely stuffed and satisfied for a long time; it turned out to be the last excellent breakfast we had on East-Prussian soil. Not long thereafter, the kindly host was seized; he's probably starved to death in the Urals.

The H[eilsberger]. *Dreieck* is an extensive region that the *Wehrmacht* has equipped for years with modern fortifications, but to the untrained eye there exists nothing of the sort. The landscape hasn't been changed anywhere. Where and how we, as reinforcements, are supposed to be of use is a mystery to everyone. When we report at the local command stations, they are discussing the same thing — they are unable to find anything for us to do. Personally, I get the impression from one of these discussions that they just don't want to sacrifice us old men senselessly. So they are pleased if we look for something to do in other, less dangerous places.

As in earlier instances, I suggest they put us in charge of the refugees. If we are vested with the appropriate authority, I argue, we will be able to be of some real assistance. This suggestion was always greeted happily by the *Wehrmacht* section heads, and furthermore, it was always acknowledged as a good and necessary use of manpower. But the Party had a different viewpoint — for them, this had nothing to do with the people. It was victory that was important, and victory that was demanded.

So we marched on farther north towards the coast. The destination is B[raunsberg; Braniewo]. With every mile, the stream of refugees continues to swell, adding more and more people who long to reach the Vistula. We push along herds of cattle as well. Their numbers grow, and soon hundreds or thousands liven up the snow-covered fields beside the streets. Later we found out that this East-Prussian cattle, accurately characterized as Germany's most valuable breeding stock, were driven into mine fields and destroyed —

For a breeder and lover of animals, this march provided many dreadful images. The highest quality of purebred animals — their udders swollen and filled to bursting. They are bellowing, tormented by pain, and no one milks them. Others can't move their legs because their hooves have been worn through. Others with broken legs make several useless attempts to stand up. In the meantime, one or another bears a calf, but the young animal, as well as its mother, will probably not live very long.

Trains of refugees and hospital trains are stopped still on the railway. All sections of track are completely jammed, but luckily Ivan remains a bad pilot. Otherwise, a large part of the population, as well as a large number of the wounded, could have been killed.

In B[raunsberg]. we poke through the remnants of other *Volkssturm* units. A new inventory of troops is to be taken soon, and it will all be diligently recorded. There will be pompous stirring speeches. One roll-call will follow another. Confusion will reign, and it will all be done as if something were actually being done. One fat, uniformed, and deluded Party member follows on the heels of another. They are extremely self-confident — they have victory in the bag, sure as day — and then they disappear in their enormous luxury cars.

The city is filled to the brim with units from all parts of the *Wehrmacht*, and with refugees as well. Many of the refugees wanted to reach the spit of land across the frozen [*Frisches*] *Haff* [Zalew Wiślany],[66] completing their journey to the west. Here, too, I meet acquaintances searching for relatives, but no one has any advice to give. We all feel equally helpless and forsaken.

Commands blare out through the loudspeakers. Posters are put up telling us that anyone who leaves his unit without authorization will be shot or hanged immediately. Every German, aged sixteen and over, must report immediately to the nearest section office. The enemy has been pounded to destruction at this place and that place — victory is ours, etc.

No one listens to it anymore, but no one dares to speak his mind either, for the *Gestapo* and the *SS* are everywhere. Everyone has had too much — it's always "onwards," "farther," "in a little while," but where is the assurance or the certainty? There's an amazing amount of air activity; the anti-aircraft guns fire. Sometimes a small rain of enemy volleys makes it through, but there aren't any bombs. B[raunsberg]. is a good, valuable target, and the Russian pilots figured that secret out a few days later, after we had left. Then, as the old soldier's saying goes, the city was completely blown to pieces.[67]

The diocesan town of F[rauenburg; Frombork]., which lay close

---

66. The spit that encloses the *Frisches Haff* into which the Vistula river flows.
67. *Zur Sau machen*, an idiom that literally means "to make into a sow, or pig."

to the [*Frisches*] *Haff*, was under fire from bomber planes when we got there. We stole around into the houses on the edge of the city, and had the bad luck of coming near our anti-aircraft position, which attracted bombs like a magnet. The gunner crew of skillful, funny young men held back nothing in their motivating barrage of curses and exclamations. Heavy chunks of earth whistled by our ears; old legs became amazingly agile.

Then the old heavy walls of the Cathedral became a relatively safe cover for the next few hours. In the falling darkness, I took a few men and went out searching for all of our things and the other groups. The horses and carts were found and assigned without any great problem, yet finding the scattered soldiers was more difficult and time-consuming. The enemy wasn't anywhere in the area, so it wasn't likely there would be any clashes. The commanders decided that they would remain in F[rauenburg]., near the active troops, while the other troops should be transferred to W., a train station only a few kilometers away that lay directly on the banks of the [*Frisches*] *Haff*.

I go there as well. On the way, at the foot of a steep slope downstream from the diocesan town, I find a well-camouflaged, armored train. In lengthening intervals it's sending its deep, heavy greetings in the direction of T[olkemit; Tolkmicko].-E[lbing; Elblag]. Between the train and our destination is a brickyard where we salvage some things to eat — the four men there wouldn't be eating for a long time. Ivan probably surprised them right at the beginning of the meal. Four quick shots, and then four bodies frozen like stone, well preserved by the cold. In the adjoining room under a table, there's a worker with a crushed skull; for lack of time we don't search for any more victims.

Among other things in W., we come across a small supply depot with some abandoned living space above. With the official Party seal on the doors, it was closed to the ordinary person. I had the door forced open immediately, and inside we find all the big-wigs' most treasured possessions. Everything is piled up nicely and neatly; there are boxes stacked to the ceiling, filled with oil paintings, books, rugs, fabrics, silver, porcelain, and many other things. Except for the furniture that appears useful and worth keeping, everything else is tossed to the back and out the window or into the hallway.

The furnaces are working. Soon they are warm — we have found ourselves good quarters. And with warm furnaces, we can better relax and let the events come to us. One dispatch rider after another appears from the "headquarters" F[rauenburg]. The masters there demand things that perhaps they could expect from a regular unit, but they just leave me cold. It's too bad that we don't have a telephone. It's so much easier to get things off your chest on the telephone, things that you would never dare put on paper. Previous experiences are already affecting my reaction to the orders. You think and say, "You all know what you can do with...."

We're supposed to learn the details of the area just like that, and produce a few heroic deeds in the process. And we're expected to write up detailed hourly reports and deliver it to them — "Yes, you will get everything you want, completely in order, but before anything else, send us our truck of rations because we're all so hungry here that we might just black out, and then everything else will catch up with us too."

The wooded area reaches right up next to the town, and practically reeks of Ivan. Almost all of the men are on guard duty, for to have single guards here is impossible. I quickly get in touch with the *Wehrmacht* at the nearby farms and receive a dependable promise to provide the support I need in the surrounding area. Therefore, I don't have to send out any scouting parties. Happily, we also live off some of the troops there for a while — that is, I take some advances of food and supplies that hold us over until our own supplies come, which one day they actually do, allowing us to take care of ourselves.[68]

The Russians push in deeper, and again they grow unpleasantly bold. Skirmishes with the outposts become much more frequent and are getting closer. The traffic on the [*Frisches*] *Haff* is the same day and night. We can't see much though; it's too far away. But at night we can hear more clearly, and sometimes we see a brief glow of fire flare up on the main route of the F[rauenburg]. crossing. The distance from there to the spit of land is about twenty kilometers.

68. i.e., they no longer had to depend on the regular forces, the *Wehrmacht*, for supplies.

At some places the sheet of ice started to weaken, due to thawing and the exceedingly heavy traffic. As a result, heavy vehicles were forbidden to cross, but nevertheless a number of them tried and broke through the ice and sank. Few people were saved. Detours were made around the places they fell in, but at night the markers couldn't always be seen in time. There was more artillery fire, a terrifying chaos, a river of refugees on the crumbling ice, which claimed many more victims, a number that would have been difficult to estimate.[69]

Ivan has long since figured out that this region contains some heavy German artillery, which he is unable to find, and yet which attracts his scouting parties like a magnet, leaving us not a minute of rest. Still the armored train continues to send its heavy greetings — it remains faultlessly camouflaged but is no longer able to change its position. It has been surrounded, and the crew has resolved to hold out as long as possible — until their last shell.

A ranger's lodge, where a German unit is holed up, is caught by surprise. Every man in the unit is killed. We have the task of resolving the matter — that is, we must raid the Ivans there, and, if possible, bring back a few prisoners. But the lair was empty. There was nothing else to do, and the dead couldn't tell us anything. The battle had probably been quick and decisive. A bag, filled to bursting, is dangling from a pile of wood. I examine it more closely, and what a joy for everybody — I find about eight hundred cigarettes and some other tobacco. The Ivans had probably missed it.

A line of refugees is moving along the railway embankment. There are old women, old men, children, and some adolescents. All the signs of terror are written in their faces as they tell their stories. We read it in the children's faces contorted by pain and fear, in the tense limbs, in the crazed glassy looks of the old men and the old women.

Some tanks had suddenly driven into the small city of

---

69. See *Dokumentation der Vertreibung der Deutschen aus Ost-Mittelevropa* edited by Theodor Schieder (Band 1, Teil I [1953] p. 110) for another first-hand description of fleeing Germans making the perilous and agonizing crossing of the frozen *Frisches Haff* at the same time Thiel was making his crossing in early 1945.

T[olkemit?]. Afterwards came the hordes of Russians, who rounded up all of the remaining inhabitants. Then the girls over six were raped right there on the spot, along with the women, even the old women. Many of them died, unable to withstand that torture repeated twenty or thirty times over. These people to whom we now talked, however, had been able to save themselves when the German tanks pressed forward.

One of our dispatch riders has positive proof that a Russian T34 tank is moving in the direction of the brickyard. The region there is hilly and wooded. I grab myself a pair of *Panzerfäuste* and hit the road immediately. The thrill of the hunt also arouses G., who has only one arm. He accompanies me and soon we have the tank within earshot, and then we can see it, but it's still too far to shoot. Yet there is no possibility of getting any closer without being seen.

The tank starts moving again. It moves in our direction, as if it has discovered us and wants to run us over. Then it stops again and turns the turret towards the [*Frisches*] *Haff*, shooting at an uncertain target. The distance is still too far; a decent shot is not possible. Either he's going to roll up even closer to us, we'll be discovered, and then a quick burst of machine gun fire will quiet us for good, or he's going to change direction and we'll lose him. For some time now, I've had half of him in the notch of my sights. I adjust to a little bit over the turret, and — nothing. Failure!

No other big-game hunt has ever made my heart beat like it does now. My companion passes me the other "pendulum," which I unscrew with flying fingers and make sure it's working. In the meantime we hear the tank's engine start to race across from us — again he's in sight — but this time he's going full steam ahead. My shot is too low, but rips off the giant's chain tracks as well as a piece from the back. Then the crew pours out of the turret.

We have no other weapons except our pistols, and so we start moving backwards as quickly as possible, running to the highway and towards a German *Sturmgeschütz*.[70] Its crew is leaving the box at that moment; they've used their last drop of fuel and have to get out

---

70. A self-propelled assault gun.

of there. A cloud of smoke comes from the direction of the T34. Later we find out that it was burning because it had just been destroyed, along with its crew, by an anti-tank defense that was well-camouflaged in the reeds.

Our position here has become meaningless — we receive an order to go to the spit nearby and gather in D[anzig]. It was high time to give the command to withdraw; more and more frequently the men were making that decision for themselves and disappearing. The old method of getting home, by self-inflicted wounds, was now checked strictly and punished severely. One evening we were standing ready to march off, checking again that we had taken all measures necessary to carry through a silent, nighttime departure — the horses are not allowed to lose their "shoe sacks"[71] — the wheels of the carts are wrapped up as well — nothing is allowed to clatter against the baggage, etc.

The search unit goes to the front. It is made up of four men, each with a long pole, with which they thoroughly check over a wide strip of land for possible holes or crevices. Then follow the replacements, the man with the compass, the columns, and the baggage train. Along with two MPs, I bring up the rear.

After a few hundred meters, the noises can't be ignored any longer — fire is coming from behind. Luckily for us Ivan is shooting aimlessly; it's either too short to reach us or it's landing to our sides. We start marching faster. Those of us behind have a hard time communicating, and then one cart in front of us swerves a little bit, and then the other. Two of our men have been hit — they lie before us, groaning in their blood, but our shouts can't make the wagons in front of us stop. So I grab the whistle and briefly turn on the flashlight, even though the gleam of light will certainly give us away. But the drivers understand, and so instead of making things worse, they come to a halt.

The doctor arrives and cares for both men. They are now on the wagons, which are moving as quickly as possible again. It seems as though a butterfly flutters onto the side of my neck. I grab after it, and I feel that the collar on my jacket has been ripped open — but once more I was lucky. Ivan is firing again, this time in longer

---

71. Sacks on their hooves to muffle the sound.

intervals. Some of the explosions land pretty damned near, but we continue to march doggedly into the night.

The lensatic compass doesn't always lead us straight ahead, and here in the back we can only faintly hear the regular sounds of searching, which come from the poles in front. We can tell that we're not moving alone on this route — noises next to us attest to that. Could they be Russian scouting parties? With every moment, it feels as if we're going to be attacked.

I shout to an indistinguishable "something" at my right, and several voices answer at the same time. They are five soldiers, pushing and pulling a sled and swearing like crazy, happy to find some friends and to figure out with certainty where they are. They've been moving for a few hours, but most of that time was spent wandering in circles. They had been ordered to bring the sled's passengers to safety — there was a landowner with her baby, and two other children under five. They had lost one of their horses to shrapnel from a shell, and the other to a broken leg.

And now they think they can hand over this wearisome "freight" to us, and escape quickly without any burden. I inform them otherwise — I convince them to get into the column and to continue pulling the sled. Two of the children are crying incessantly, and the mother is apparently either mute or dead. I am unable to make out anything under the furs and the blankets. Finally at daybreak, the repetitious screaming grows silent. The soldiers are despicable, so much so that I don't let them out of the range of my pistol — then we reach the spit, and in haste I was only able to wish the unfortunate woman well for the rest of her journey. By that time, her baby and one of the children had died.

Now I have the time and the light to examine my right leg more closely, which has been burning for some time. The leg of my boot has two holes in it, big enough to stick a small finger through, and I find some dried and crusty blood. There are similar rips in my jacket, and my pants are torn open as well, as if they had gotten hooked on some barbed wire — but again I am lucky.

There's a huge operation at the spit — here are the first people we see hanged, of both sexes, dangling from the trees. Their "offenses" are clearly visible to everybody, written on cardboard fastened around their necks or on their legs. Initially we found one or another case that seized our attention, but later, when even soldiers of all ranks were being hanged, no one looked anymore at all. We only asked ourselves why one so well-equipped as a soldier had let himself be killed? Had these men lost all of their energy, along with all their good sense? Why wouldn't any of our army commanders — to save us from drowning completely — shoot down the madman at the helm of our nation?

On the spit, in the houses of the resort town K[ahlberg; Krynica Morska]., great streams of refugees are milling about. The bakers and the butchers are not allowed to sell any of their supplies unless they receive marks, and so the people suffer from hunger. When we start marching again, we find them beyond the ditches on the side of the road, frozen or starved. Some move along, without baggage and wearing threadbare, half-shoes with frozen feet. Others move along meter by meter with their families, in cars that are nearly destroyed. Then we see the limousines with big-wigs and spruced-up whores, and the *Wehrmacht* vehicles with the women and girls they picked up on the way. Though we should have, no one dared shoot up the tires on those vehicles — court-martials are handed out quickly — you only had to search out the tree.

For a night and a day we get room and board at the well known concentration camp of S[tutthof; Sztutowo]. Here, too, refugees and *Wehrmacht* units are streaming around everywhere. The command of the camp is in the hands of the SS, and the prisoners have long since been transported westwards. As I am negotiating with the administrative offices for a place for us to stay, a woman refugee silently lays a bundle, rolled up in clothes, on the camp leader's desk. She moves away, just as quietly. A secretary pulls the cloth back, and then her hands tremble a little as she carries the bundle into the adjoining room. It was a dead child. She assures me despondently that the incident was not unusual.

We didn't want to remain in the overheated, overfilled, foul-smelling shacks, where clothes are hung to dry, where chilblain and wounds are washed and taken care of, where crying children and wailing women are all wandering around — an ice-cold plane hangar would be more pleasant than this hovel.

D[anzig].'s big city bustle is amazing; everything seems to be going as if it were peace time. The people gape at us like at animals in the zoo. Do they still have all their senses? Is Ivan really only about thirty kilometers away? Here they still don't know the word "escape."

A short time later this beautiful city, perhaps the reason for the war,[72] was blown to bits. There must have been some indescribable scenes when the KdF[73] steamship, "*W. Gustloff*,"[74] ran into a mine or was torpedoed when it was overladen with refugees. But the inhabitants of D[anzig]. still didn't believe there was any danger, for the propaganda continued successfully to suggest the opposite.

My "unit" had grown so small I had little more to do than hand out the weapons and the ammunition we had brought along — and then afterwards I could be "free" by myself. Should I flee? Disappear in all the chaos and be a coward? No. I wanted to see Ivan again, to get even with him, to have a respectable conclusion. Even a blind man had to recognize that everything was coming to an end — perhaps it was possible to escape to Sweden or Denmark, but otherwise there was only the path to the front, and there a clean end was questionable.

Unfortunately, the field SS was moving out on that same day, and the opportunity to flee was lost. So instead I was assigned to a replacement battalion in N[eustadt?; Wejherowo]., and luckily for me, the battalion was at the end of its course. The small scratch on my leg was not much of a difficulty, and the doctor was taking care

---

72. There was great friction between Poland and Germany after World War I, partly because of the Polish Corridor, a narrow stretch of land ceded to Poland in the Treaty of Versailles. This strip of land provided Poland access to the Baltic Sea, but separated Germany from East Prussia. In March of 1939, Germany demanded the cession of the Free City of Danzig as well as an additional German corridor across the Polish corridor. Poland refused and asked France and Britain to help defend them against German aggression. They agreed, and on September 1, 1939, Germany attacked Poland.

73. KdF is an abbreviation for "*Kraft durch Freude*," which means "strength through joy." It was a Nazi scheme that provided the lower classes with an opportunity to travel on oceanliners and see things they never would have seen otherwise. Certainly there were positive aspects, but in the end the many activities became another clever means by which the Nazis could deliver their propaganda and fulfill their political agenda.

74. January 30, 1945, the *Wilhelm Gustloff* was sunk by three Russian torpedoes, killing between 7000 and 8000 people, mostly refugees, one of the greatest civilian tragedies of World War II.

of it. I didn't want to stay in bed because of it, but I hardly had to do any of the so-called "service" either.

One day there's an alarm, and the battalion commander makes a short speech. Let's get going—the Russians are around us in the forests, and they've been attacking our outposts. We set out as if we're going to engage in an exercise. Along with my unit, I move into a position that has already been trenched, a little west of the city. The wide, concrete arterial road runs through the zone, and a deep anti-tank ditch runs behind us. We stand in the foxholes on the ridge of the trenches, and soon we're freezing like little puppies. We had taken off without our coats and without lunch. It gets dark, and for hours now a strong wind has been racing along, cutting us through to the bone.

On the street there's commotion coming from all types of *Wehrmacht* machines. Refugees have been pushed to the side, and now they're standing helplessly next to their vehicles, some of which are tipped over. Others abandon everything and try to get away— they move faster without any burden. But in what direction are they to go? I can't tell whether their instincts are leading them the right way—in any case, part of them is heading westwards, and another eastwards, and there is no one who can tell them what to do.

We're freezing miserably, standing in fox-holes as if we're nailed in, and still nothing is to be seen of Ivan. But then the first salvos howl by and explode in the area. Is he looking for us or for the supply line?[75] And now more movement compounds the chaos. A few PKW break out from the roads and try to move faster in the open fields. There are teams of horses dragging carts filled with baggage— they follow the example of the cars, but our anti-tank ditches keep anything from crossing. The cars are abandoned, and the people run back to the turmoil in the streets.

Right in front of us there are two baggage wagons, and the horses are freezing—they try to get back to the road by themselves, but they flip over the carts and dump the loads into the snow. I let one man leave his cover to free the animals from their plight. At that

75. The German word here is *Rollbahn*, which in this instance has a meaning specific to the Eastern Front during World War II: they were temporary roads or runways constructed for the transportation of supplies.

time he examines the contents, and then reappears full of joy, loaded down with chocolate, salami, and alcohol. We are in great need of these things — never has something been eaten so fast and with such a hearty appetite, and even more amazing was how ravenously we guzzled the drinks.

The next "scouting party" searches the other cart, and soon we have a stockpile of these wonderful things. There are loads of tobacco products and powdered milk as well, so a lot of stuff can be given out to our compatriots.

A few hours later the firing from the tanks and the anti-tank guns has eased up considerably, and the stream on the road has thinned out as well. A few blazes flare up. To both our left and right sides we can hear machine guns a good distance away. A new report comes in — a large number of enemy tanks should be expected on and next to the street, heading in the direction of N[eustadt?]. Shortly afterwards we receive an order to withdraw immediately from our position and move up to the left. In the meantime the enemy tanks have rolled on forward, and we haven't yet reached the edge of the woods when they flood us with their blasts.

Ivan has taken control of the area. Our leadership either doesn't want to, or is unable to put up any further resistance. I get permission to creep up on one of the tanks that's rolling nearby, but unfortunately, since no possibility of cover is available, I don't get up as close as I would like. The thrill of the hunt overcame any logical thought — I held the gun high, and the shot shattered the chain tracks. The crew flew out of the tank like greased lightening. Next, the second shot landed just like the first one, too low. Then we really had to get our legs moving — the other tank crews were furious, understandably, and they generously scattered their little gifts into the region. The commander had watched the scene, and despite the "miss," he was extraordinarily pleased.

The attackers kept firing on the city. Three of our heavy anti-aircraft guns destroyed a nice row of their tanks, which were advancing from our side. Our guns were extremely well camouflaged, and they continued to fire down to their last shell. We occupy and then withdraw, first from one and then from another position. We run into small enemy groups, then find ourselves "blessed" by the

guns — we chalk up the casualties. Most disturbing are the marks-
men who do their job too damned well —

Apparently we are completely surrounded, and the situation
seems to be pretty damned hopeless. The leaders are getting
drunk — they lose their composure, along with the last bit of trust
they had from the men. A first sergeant (a front-weathered veteran,
highly decorated, wounded in battle several times) is given command
of the neighboring company. He asks me for accommodations in the
sick-bay. My astonishment grows even greater as he thoughtfully
shakes a hand-grenade in his hand, and pulls the pin. "I've had
enough of this shit. We're all going to hell here; I want to see the
wife and kid again one more time — you will certainly understand
and arrange my evacuation." He moves away a few steps, and there's
an explosion. The bundle of nerves is still alive — he groans,
suffering heavy leg injuries. I call it an accident and arrange the
evacuation. I like his handshake about as much as I like the order to
take over his company.

In truth our positions are intolerable, and there's nothing sensi-
ble that can be made from the reports we get on the radio. Apparently a senior command no longer exists. The principle is to act
independently. We therefore decide to try to escape the unavoidable
imprisonment — we choose the one path that is left us to D[anzig].,
and try to get through to the units there. The SS that was stationed
near us has already cleared out. We have nothing that could even
come close to countering the fire that rains down on us, heavier and
fiercer by the hour. The casualties rise.

The familiar words "until the last man" no longer seem to make
an impression on anyone except for a few commanding officers heavily under the influence of alcohol. Thus a staggering first lieutenant,
who tries to chase the men back to a ridiculous position, is simply
bumped off with few pistol shots by a sergeant — right before a
group of lined-up men.

Flames engulf the barracks, and though I want to go in and
gather up the most important of my personal things, my attempt to
enter comes to ruin. In the kitchen building, however, everything is
still intact, and there I manage to find some cooked meals and
plenty of other food as well. The first two ladles-full are rendered

inedible when plaster starts falling from the ceiling — so instead I pull a few sausages from a pole and take to my heels.

A line of soldiers disappears into the burning city, wearing recently acquired civilian suits. Endless vehicles and columns surge down the wide, tarred road to G[otenhafen; Gdynia]. and D[anzig]. They move forward as quickly as possible, with everything on its last reserves — animals, gas, and muscles. It is night. Ivan finds us, and at longer intervals he fires into the throng. The wreckage is moved into the ditches as quickly as possible, for any moment the tanks could appear from the flank and then it would all be over. During the course of the night, all contact with our own men is lost. Here everyone is moving on his own.

I get a place on a towing vehicle from an artillery unit — a chance gift. The heavy engine provides some good warmth. It's only too bad that we're not heading westwards as was planned, finally to get out of this hopeless mess. Soon I'm sleeping like a dead man. In G[otenhafen]. (earlier a Polish seaport) we run out of gas. I haven't had the slightest bit of training when it comes to artillery, so I'm completely useless here. Well-rested, I squeeze my way through to a meeting point where I hope to find at least a small part of my battalion.

One air-raid after another comes down over the harbor. Our anti-aircraft fire isn't bad — many an Englishman or American (one can never tell one from the other) spins down burning, or swings back and forth in his parachute.

Either I am here much too early, or I am the only one from the old unit who reports. In any case I let myself be taken again, and then I am assigned to a new unit composed of the scattered soldiers in the area. The next day we are put to a march and head towards the front. Everything about this is too similar to my old memories of the *Volkssturm*, even though words like "command" and "composure" etc. can describe these regular troops. There are certainly no more "boys" stuck inside these uniforms. The old front-weathered veterans know all the tricks — yet they are dulled, apathetic, and thoroughly exhausted. They held on to the Courland[76] to the end, but they

---

76. A region on the Baltic Sea.

know that it's coming down to the last battle, and there doesn't seem to be any way out of this trap.

The enemy navy fires its heaviest caliber guns. Numerous bodies are hanging from ropes in the trees. Their air force joins fire with their artillery — they bombard our anti-aircraft and anti-tank emplacements, which are regularly growing thinner. But our guns continue to fight, down to the last shell, and then they are blown up.

The night finds us in the forest in a pair of neighboring bunkers, made from thick concrete and connected by narrow gauge railways. It's dark, damp, and bitter cold. We have no straw or any place to sit down. Not a swig of warm coffee, and not any prospect of getting something to eat. We stand there cursing and almost freeze to death. After a brief time I hear the first, and then several rifle shots in the "salon." Hand and arm injuries — the idiots probably think they'll be bandaged up and then evacuated, and so on — yeah, shit. Perhaps you'll be lucky and won't get any cramps from your wound — but Ivan will get you like this anyway.

Nevertheless, in this crowd it is possible a gun could go off accidentally. But a medical orderly can't be found anywhere; there's not even a need for the category anymore.

The next day my mood barometer sinks below zero when I am made the temporary platoon leader — and then I'm supposed to go occupy a small zone. In a barn we have a large storeroom of weapons and ammunition at our disposal, but unfortunately, it turns out that because of rust and drifting sand, less than ten percent of them are usable. And only a very few machine guns can be used as well, and the ammunition that's strapped to them is lying piled in the sand and the mud. No extra barrels can be found either, and there's even less of the all important oil and grease. With the best pieces, we move into a rolling hilly area and take our position; I still have to check over each particular sentry post and maintain contact with the command post.

At a farm there is a potato steamer, which soon is working and providing us with some good hot nourishment. Shortly thereafter comes a wonderful sign — the food drivers turn up too, giving away a large number of their treasures. Unfortunately the soup is ice cold, but to make up for it, there is bread, sausage, butter, and smoking materials, which are always accepted and taken happily.

At the beginning everything is calm and quiet. At dark there's the Russian's night concert again — it comes from gigantic loud-speakers, delighting us with soldier songs like "Lili Marleen," then playing popular hits and marches. Between the songs an "ordinary man" speaks the same types of diatribes we hear from "Jupp" (Goebbels).[77] Then the "true" military briefing follows, and a pair of our former comrades, now deserters, praise the Russian paradise with glowing colors. At the end we hear the propagandist with the usual, repeated declarations — "Come over to us in masses — bring along your mess tins and your spoons — thousands of naked women are waiting for you — in ten minutes you'll be having sex."

During the afternoon hours of the next day, Ivan floods us with a fierce bombardment. Then he attacks, but we greet him when he's still a good distance away and inflict severe casualties. He postpones the next assault, and "softens us up" again. On top of it all, our own artillery fire makes some "mistakes" (the attacker still isn't at our trenches). But all our cursing isn't helping anything, and doesn't make the casualties any less severe.

The SS keeps hold of the zone to the left. Ivan attacks there and suffers heavy losses. If he breaks through there, we'll have him at our back and to our flank. We can't see across the terrain, but we can hear them and we guess, unfortunately correctly, that the zone has been overrun. And then a little while later we hear that a counterattack by the SS was successful, and that Ivan has been pushed back.

We can take a deep breath now, and hope for quiet with the coming night. Tanks of all sizes move in front of the main-battle line, as if they were summoned for a parade. It's clear that the guys there know they're now in control of the situation, despite their heavy losses. And we know that our light arms have no more mean-ing here — yes, our *Panzerfäuste* will undoubtedly knock open some holes, but they will never be able to hold back the flood. We lack the heavy defense weaponry.

---

77. Young Josephs were often called *Juppchen*. This reference to "Jupp" is obviously a deroga-tory reference to Goebbels whose given name was Joseph.

On the other side, a few brazen figures come out from under their cover. Apparently they feel safe so far away, but we pick them off for as long as the rifles can be kept primed in the fine drifting sand. We use jackets and tarpaulins to protect them as if they're precious treasures. We hunted, and I was able to record a good number of hits. My men were more than a little surprised, and they came to be very keen spotters for me. After all, the old woodsman and hunter understood something of the business here.

Contrary to his normal tendencies, Ivan attacks today under poor visibility for a second time. Once more he makes it up to the edge of the trenches, but we have stick[78] and pineapple hand grenades by the ton. Again they save a hopeless situation, and now the wounded can finally be taken to the back.

At the break of day the engines roar up on the other side — there's the sound of spinning chain-tracks everywhere. The command is given to clear out the area, and again all hell is unleashed. In leaps and bounds we work ourselves from one crater to another — they give us momentary cover and the opportunity to wipe the dirt from our eyes. We move along in that way, separated from one another. Everyone pays attention to his instincts and advances farther alone.

I land in a positional trench on a pile of fallen Russian and SS men. The bombardment has grown even heavier — a steel broom sweeps over the ground. It's necessary to remain low to the ground; we are only able to crawl along now. We get used to temporarily holding our noses among those who have long since moved to the eternal hunting grounds.

In the curve of the trench I see two SS men struggling to put a new strap of ammo into their SMG. One of them stands up just a little bit, whereupon his head and steel helmet are both torn off. The other one had noticed me earlier, and now he makes a motion to follow him. We crawl farther along the trench, and at the next bend we run into another machine gun that continues to shoot. These boys have nerves and a little bit of luck as well, and thus they manage to provide some cover for the retreating survivors.

---

78. Stick hand grenades are also known as "potato mashers" in British army slang.

Then there follows another section of trench without any dead, and then yet another stretch where friends and foes lie on top of one another in several layers. We reach a so-called command post, which even has radio contact with the rear. Here I receive the first reprimand in a long time, delivered humorously. He asks me why I'm not wearing a steel helmet — I tell him it would get torn up.

Anyway, we hurriedly size each other up. Then I get a light for my cigarette and a short situation report, along with good wishes for the future. He's part of a mobile unit that has to go wherever the situation stinks; he is uncertain how the conditions will change over the next few hours. With the help of his low-flying aircraft, Ivan gets the exact range of his targets. And then his tanks calmly plow and crush our trenches, one after the other, along with the last of our now weak forces.

Behind the nearby mountain-ridge, it is a bit calmer. The fire is considerably lighter here, and no tanks are seen at all. Instead, the air traffic is much more lively. Scattered soldiers from all branches of the service are wandering around, and everyone is confused and completely exhausted. I join a group that is on its way to its command post. It still has some weapons left, and therefore has kept its composure. "Council" is held in a farm reasonably far from the shooting; they have radio contact here as well. Even lists of names are printed out, casualty lists amended, new groups assembled, etc.

At night we move into position. I share the standard foxhole with a private first class and a sergeant. We are supposed to stay in close contact with the command post and with the neighboring sector. It was the 28th of March, 1945, an unforgettable day, and at dawn we start to get a picture of the area around us. The lighter it got, the easier it was to recognize the hopeless conditions. We hear the usual tank sounds, and the first low flying aircrafts thunder immediately over our positions. No dispatch courier comes from the rear, which was at least 20 minutes away.

I make a quick sketch along with a short report. The private first class takes them and gets on his way. At the same time a man rumbles out of the neighboring hole, and, given the circumstances, comes to me to get commands. But just at this moment the dance begins — the orchestra is represented by different intensities of sound. We couldn't spot an opening anywhere in the range of the binoculars. There was one tank and then another tank driving around still far away, uncamouflaged and acting completely sure of themselves.

We get smeared by many multiple rocket launchers and rocket mortars — and all hell is unleashed. My watch shows exactly 0830 hours. We kneel or crouch very close to each other, and smoke one cigarette after another. Again and again we shovel ourselves free from the piles of sand which fill our hole and make our legs numb. There is an old front-weathered veteran beside me, and he swears to me repeatedly that he has never experienced a bombardment like this before. He also assures me that this will be the last one.

The courier didn't make it back. The apathetic crouch with their legs buried in the sand. Is it not finally coming, that direct hit that would alleviate everything? Not a damn soul is going to make it out of here. Will we be captured? And maybe even wounded in the process? No, they will never get me. The old Mauser can still spit out a good seven rounds — one of them has to be saved; one round will be sufficient. So supposedly Christ doesn't permit you to kill yourself? Well is it better to let yourself be cut up alive by Ivan? In this hell there isn't supposed to be any scruples. I have only the one penetrating desire, and that is to keep whatever finger strength is necessary.... With this thought I begin to calm down.

The sergeant (I don't even know his name) asks me not to forget his sister's address. There I will find his wife as well, and I should only say that ... etc. When I smile towards him he assures me that, without a doubt, I will make it through — because he has a feeling for it, and also because I have strong nerves. There is no point trying to understand single words. We're shouting at one another — we have been submerged in this inferno for a long time now.

The gas-mask case is a tightly guarded treasure because it always contains tobacco products instead of gas-masks. Even now the contents again prove themselves to be wonderful. What would one do without a smoke?

Again my whole life flashes through my mind; I can picture all the most important events. I would have liked to have talked to one person or another, at least to have waved to my favorite, or most devoted relatives. I would have liked to have known the reason for this global conflagration, what would be left, and what the human animal could be planning for the future.

The Russian artillery shoots through the air (perhaps it is also ours; it is impossible to hear and tell one from the other), scattering whole arsenals of steel over the ground. The six-barreled rocket mortars, which the Russians stole from us and now use themselves, vibrate like donkeys getting ready to neigh. The other multiple rocket launchers have a different, characteristic wail and a good spread. The artillery gun spits out about 30 shots at the same time, and then there are the mortars of all different strengths with a stunning, deep action. Everything that was invented by human minds to kill one another — except for gas — spits and pukes all at once.

The fire stops at exactly 0930 hours. As quickly as possible I move the sand and dig out the three *Panzerfäuste* again, which had been buried for a while now. I am also able to rouse the person next to me, and get him to prepare himself for his last journey. The third man has probably already had it — he doesn't even react to a kick.

The low-flying aircraft now ring out with machine guns as well. Tanks rattle with constantly changing courses, firing into the region in every direction. There is no defense whatsoever coming from our side. We are ruined, without exception. But no, several hundred meters to the right I see a huge, familiar flash, followed immediately by an explosion. Bulls-eye. A second trail of fire comes from the same place, and again a small fortress is ablaze. This gunner is a talented young man. Concealed, somewhat in the rear — another mushroom cloud follows a successful explosion.

Apparently not all of the old, proven hands are finished yet either. In a short time a half dozen of the monster tanks are in flames. The others lurch around in the area from side to side, starting to bombard or run over every little bulge of earth they can find. The chance to get a good shot has never been as good as it is here. And there's nothing like letting them have it.

The sergeant can't help anymore. His head is buried between his arms and he is crouched down like a dead man. Not twenty paces away one of the monsters rolls past, nicely revealing its side.

Others were even closer, but weren't positioned as favorably for my shot. I watched only half of the explosion, and then pulled my head in and automatically fished for the other *Panzerfaust*. As I did so, I was knocked to the side by a force I did not see, and I lost consciousness.

III

Russian Captivity

I have often wondered whether the impact from some kind of shell knocked down that wall, at the same time throwing me up in the air, or whether a tank's treads, while crossing over my hole, simply didn't press it tightly enough together. I don't know how long I lay there, in or next to the hole, but when I came to I was stripped down to my underwear in the midst of a number of Russians. They seemed to be saying something or issuing some kind of command.

I couldn't hear anything, and my eyes were gummed up with sand and dirt. I slowly recovered my ability to think, and then I too clearly realized that I had been unable to avoid the hated and feared captivity. Their guys are standing at a respectful distance with their submachine guns aimed and ready. Why does no one pull the trigger? They've undressed me completely — there's no trace of my wristwatch, the Mauser, my knife, my lighter, or my boots. One of them hands me my wallet, from which I later recover the pictures of my children, as well as several large bills in a secret compartment. All of my identification cards etc. are gone.

I was told later that at that time Ivan received 10 rubles for every prisoner he brought in — perhaps that was enough to keep them from finishing me off. I am given a tunic that came from a fallen soldier. Pants and shoes were in great demand and not necessary for me, so in that state, off we go towards the east. Ten meters away two Russians have their weapons cocked and ready to fire.

At a farm I come upon the first of my fellow-captives,[79] but we are not permitted to exchange a single word. Here I also see the first

---

79. The word Thiel uses is *Leidensgenossen*, literally "fellow-sufferers."

uniformed women soldiers[80]—they make a ghastly impression on us, but they don't spit and bite. They seem only to occupy themselves with their eternal cigarettes and the captured watches and jewelry. It's impossible to study them in greater detail—a rifle barrel bores its way into my back.

We move farther through the softened slush and come to a small town, past firing mortars and a Signal Corps laying down its lines. There seems to be some type of command post in a crowded farmhouse. I am standing in the washroom with my face to the wall, two Russians at my back with their guns cocked. A few other captives arrive, and they look like walking death. They simply stretch themselves out on the floor. We are about six to eight men—and we are guarded by nearly twenty Russians standing behind us with their pistols drawn.

At any rate, Herr Enemy has a great deal of respect for us. An interpreter, who by his appearance is one hundred percent Jewish, announces that anyone who says a word to anyone else will be shot and killed on the spot. I signal to him that I can't hear anything, and I am generously allowed to dig the sand and dirt out of my ears. In the meantime, one after another of us is led away. I, too, have my turn, and am led into a room where three Russian officers are sitting around a table covered with maps. Behind each of them stands a Jewish individual who speaks German.

The man preceding me is being brought out. Two Russian officers have bored the barrels of their rifles into his back, and an interpreter yells, "shoot him."[81] Then I am told to step up to the table, look at the maps, and to name the exact places where our anti-air, anti-tank, and other artillery emplacements are located, and what strengths they are in each place. Every statement I make will be checked, and if I am wrong, or if I don't say anything, I will be shot like the man before me.

A cold steel barrel presses against my spine. I am going to have to disappoint these gentlemen, and I say, "If I knew something, I wouldn't say, but because I haven't seen anything, I'm not able to

80. The German is *Flintenweib*, also translated as "gunwoman." It is pejorative.
81. Apparently said in German so that the prisoners can understand.

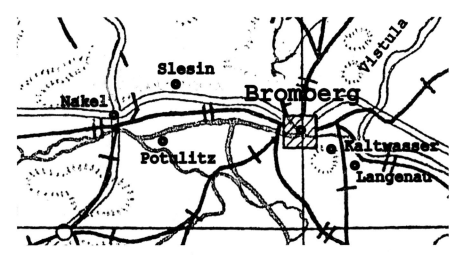

Area surrounding Bromberg. Thiel was interned in several work camps in this area: Potulitz, Kaltwasser, and Langenau. Early in that period, and after being turned over to the Poles by his Russian captors, he was tried by Polish authorities at Nakel. From a map of wartime Poland prepared by the United States Army Map Service for the Army Chief of Staff (1943).

give you any details; I have always marched during the night and night only."

"Yes, no, the map is not unfamiliar to me. I have been here for some time now, but never in the rear,[82] so I don't know anything."

"Are you an officer?"

"No, I'm from the new reinforcements."

"From the *Volkssturm*?"

"No, I've only heard of them."[83]

"Which regiment? Which division? How big was your last unit? What was your last position?"

Apparently my answers are not satisfactory. I am taken out like the man before me, and I hear the same "shoot him." The next person is being brought in.

---

82. i.e., at the command post.

83. Thiel would not be recognized as a member of the *Volkssturm* at this point, having fought mixed within regular ranks since the retreat from the Eastern Front. He may have heard that the Russians refused to treat members of the *Volkssturm* as POWs, thus brutalizing and torturing them more than regular soldiers. This might explain why he refuses to admit he was in the *Volkssturm*.

A good dozen of my fellow-captives are standing behind a barn under the same strict supervision. We are permitted to speak to one another now, but everyone has just had more or less the same experience, and we are only waiting for the final shot. And they, too, have almost nothing left to cover their bodies. We are freezing miserably; hunger gnaws at our insides. A kingdom for a cigarette —

The expected shot doesn't come and deliver us. At night we are put up in a barn, and again it is surrounded by a crowd of guards. It holds in little warmth, for the "villa" is half-way shot to pieces. An icy wind races through and despite all our best efforts, we can't find one minute of warmth or peace. In the morning we fall in and march off. Now and then in the distance there is a heavy, muffled explosion, and pillars of smoke fill the area.

Then we're hurried through the midst of some big commotion — there are tanks, trucks, cars, anti-aircraft and mortar emplacements, as well as a number of lightly harnessed horse-carts, obviously of German origin. They probably carried refugees away, but now the victors are having themselves driven around on them, along with their uniformed women soldiers (high commissars). There is just as much commotion in the air, filled for the most part by foreign planes.

Both here and later (except for the few familiar Russian-made vehicles) we see mostly American vehicles, or captured German vehicles that ran so long as their gas held out. The air is thick with the heavy-leaded fuel which we, unfortunately, had been lacking. The enormous wealth of heavy weapons, which were used to assault our barren front, is also astonishing — I think about the few useless infantry rifles we had on our side. But the most amazing thing was the enormous amount of young and robust manpower that they could quite readily sacrifice here — without leaving any gaps in the front.

The enemy was 180 million strong, and their strength was as obvious here as was their ineptitude in attack, caused by the absence of discipline, organization, and leadership. But huge quantities of the most modern heavy vehicles and weapons have come from overseas and helped the Russian bear to sharpen its claws.

In the first days we don't make any long marches, but curiously we are seldom going eastward. Is this transport doomed? Are we just supposed to be killed here somewhere? Or do they want to unite us with a larger transport? We're no longer hungry. Our stomachs must have simply passed to a stage where you cease to be conscious of an appetite.

One evening a pair of comrades uses gestures to make the guards realize that we wish to eat. The Ivans gape in astonishment. They put their heads together, dispatch a delegation, and an interpreter appears. He is told that we have not eaten for many days. After a short time, everyone receives a whole loaf of bread and a piece of heavily salted bacon. Coffee and tea weren't available, so there was vodka to wash it down, and at the end the guards fished into their pockets and gave everyone some tobacco and a part of "Pravda"[84] to roll it up with. (The ordinary Russian uses newspaper for rolling his cigarettes, while those better off, an officer or a commissar for example, use heavier paper).

The Russian was always like this: he is good-natured and gives whenever he has something, and whenever he is reminded that a man should eat once in a while. On the other hand, without hesitation, he would rob the shirt right off your back. And unfortunately, such an unpredictable thief will remain a thief forever.

On the side of the road lies a farmer who was either shot or beaten to death. It's a rare instance, for he hasn't been stripped, and his shoes come at just the right time for me. I indicate my feet to the guard, at the same time pointing to the shoes of the dead man. The guard appears to be intelligent because he got what I was saying and came to the right conclusion. So in that way I get shoes, which are actually very small but are, in any case, better than none.

During the following hours, others make the most of this generosity. There are enough dead lying around who have not yet been stripped, and whom we're allowed to undress. In this way our small unit is fitted out with motley uniforms, but at least they are clothes. The Russian military coat and cap went very well beside the German equivalents.

---

84. The Soviet newspaper that was the official publication of the Communist Party.

Guards remain for two days at the most, and then they are relieved. Every day our unit grows bigger, but, with every addition, the food rations grow smaller. Hunger and thirst torment us to a greater extent than the heavy physical demands of those guards who turn into true demons. We normally have to march from thirty to forty kilometers each day, without a drop of water, and without a bite to eat. The mounted guards are closed tightly around us. They were fed by the horse-carts that followed behind, supplied overabundantly with alcohol, and after a few hours they were relieved.

They are carrying their machine guns in front of them on short straps; between their teeth is the everpresent cigarette.[85] "*Dawai*," ("forwards" or "fast")[86] is the never-ending, hounding command. We marched down the disheveled streets in a hurried tempo, and whenever vehicles appeared we marched in the ditches, over bodies of all ages and sexes, in the slush, pools of blood, over dead animals, smashed wagons, cut up feather-beds, forced-open crates, boxes, suitcases, bags, cleaned-out or burned-out *Wehrmacht* cars, bread lying scattered about, canning jars, cans, weapons, dead and more dead etc. And it's always "*Dawai!*"

The guards had plenty of ammunition at their disposal. Anyone who stumbled out of line immediately found bullets whistling around his ears. "*Dawai!*" And then, whenever anyone in the column collapsed from exhaustion or as the result of a wound, causing a short pause, it was double time with pounding lungs. Then bullets whistled aimlessly around the drawn-in heads. Some got themselves such severe wounds that they couldn't move on any further, and then, with a quick burst, they were finished off.

"*Dawai!*" You reached for your last reserves of strength and made it to nightfall. But you never knew whether that night you would be able to lie down or rest, or whether you were going to get anything to put between your teeth. As far as it was possible we supplied ourselves with the edible things lying scattered on the way, even though a good portion of them were spoiled. A pair of raw potatoes or some *mangel-wurzel*[87] would never be left lying on the

85. The word here is *Papyros*, Eastern European and Russian slang for cigarette.
86. The correct spelling is *Davai*.
87. Root vegetable used for forage. A type of field beet.

ground even if you were thirsty — that is, if you found them and the opportunity arose to pick them up.

The LKW that approached us or overtook us from behind were usually packed with drunken soldiers of all ranks, and they could have done whatever they wanted to us. So we were lucky just to be cheered with the customary yelling of "Heetlerr kapuut!" But often during such triumphant euphoria, the clip of a pistol bestowed its favors upon us, and again there were dead or injured.

Before going to sleep at night, everyone is searched thoroughly for watches, rings, or any other valuable objects. "Do you have a ring? Do you have a watch? Then give them up or else you'll be shot." This expression became just as typical and mundane as the act of being searched. We called that "frisking."[88] Frequently some Jewish guys came in as well, and in a very businesslike manner they offered bread or bacon for watches and rings. It happened that here and there, despite the thorough checks, a wedding ring or a wristwatch remained stashed away, and then the sense-stealing[89] hunger brought these last things to light. Naturally the men were subsequently paid with a kick in the side, and then searched even more thoroughly.

One day, in a bigger, severely burnt-out town, we were going to find some accommodations — on time for once — for we were simply unable to go any further, and these guards were either more reasonable or lazier than the others. Soon an empty barn is found. We go in after a thorough "frisking." Exhausted, everyone falls down right there on the spot. Then an alarm sounds to get food — that is, food we're supposed to cook for ourselves. We pick some men who can cook, some that can do the slaughtering, and some that can milk. I choose the last task with a pair of others and am brought through the town to another farm.

On the way there's racket, howling, and music, like at a public market. Besides the refugees (who are assembled together), apparently a part of the local population remains as well. And here, in human form, the devil is having orgies. Completely undressed and

---

88. The German is *entfilzen*, a slang neologism. The term is also used to mean "de-mat" as in to "de-mat" an animal's hair or a thick lawn.
89. As in good "sense," not sensate.

half-naked women are behind the windows, in the entryways and in the yards, with every sign of horror in their eyes. Some are crazed, laughing to themselves under the effects of alcohol.

Like everywhere, there are bodies wherever one looks, but everyone is much too lethargic and too indifferent to fully grasp and understand its horror. "*Dawai!*" We are not alone and were not sent out to engage in reflection. We find a small herd of cows being looked after by several farmers, whose eyes widen when they recognize that we're soldiers. We don't need to do any milking. We receive a few buckets of milk still warm from the supply meant for the Russian provisions, along with some secret bread, sausage, and tobacco.

We can take our time with the "milking." The bread and sausage are devoured while the farmers tell us of their last weeks, and the hell that they, their wives, and their children all lived through. It was rumored much later that eyewitnesses such as these were, for the most part, killed. Those who were still capable of working were shipped behind the Urals, never to be seen again.

One of them was forced to undress his fourteen-year-old daughter, to hold her and then remain there until she died from being raped more than twenty times. Another one's mother, over seventy years old, suffered the same fate as the girl. A parish priest stayed behind with an older nun who worked in his parish. Both were undressed, laid together, and after their unsuccessful efforts,[90] the priest's genitals were crushed with bricks. The beasts then gave the poor woman a "hand" with a bayonet, and after the ensuing, repeated rape, they smashed her skull.

There was another farmer who supposedly didn't want to give away his hidden treasures — the devils shit in his mouth and forced him to swallow the feces. Another one saw some women (who hadn't yet died from anything else) choked with the severed genitals of tortured men. Other women, so far as they still looked good and had survived the tortures, were transported away in the direction of Russia.

At best, those who made it through the hell were ones who had some type of musical instrument nearby, and were able to play it. They were given special protection and provided with plenty of

90. At forced intercourse, it is assumed.

good food rations, just so long as they played. The Russian had a special weakness for music.

We return to bubbling, copper pots, carrying the milk. In the meantime a great quantity of meat is acquired from freshly-shot pigs and young cows, an amount that would have fed us for weeks to come. At the guards' command we add the milk. Potatoes are also being prepared in large quantities, and the kind hosts personally pour in salt and syrup. After a short time cooking, it can all be eaten, but in the end the strange, heavy concoction would have muddled even the healthiest of stomachs. The consequences revealed themselves quickly — heavy diarrhea and a raging thirst, and there wasn't any water because corpses and the bodies of animals were lying around everywhere. We collected the remnants of snow, and in so doing upset our stomachs completely.

With constant diarrhea, this period of marching was among the most difficult I ever experienced. Our group of men grew smaller every day. We could only suspect what happened to the comrades who were completely exhausted and broke rank to escape the marching, and with whom we then lost contact. As I already said, Ivan had more than enough ammunition at his disposal.

Every day we went in another direction, but never due east. Not even the guards knew our destination. In any case, progressing like this we will never reach Russia within the year. The German placenames and directional signs were completely gone, replaced by Russian tactical signs. This much was certain — we were being led in a circle that grew bigger each day. Perhaps our convoy wasn't worth a rail transport, or perhaps our capture wasn't recorded anywhere, and we were supposed to be wiped out on the way.

"*Dawai!*" At night, no one was allowed to leave the quarters. Our stomachs inevitably emptied themselves wherever we were lying or crouched down. The air was dreadful. During the day our wet and encrusted pants chafed and left sore, painful, skin rashes. When we had the opportunity, we exchanged the ruined clothing for others. It was only helpful for a little while, but the guards were often generous in allowing us to do so. As time went by, we grew more hardened and resigned, even to the cold steel barrel that often bored itself into our backs.

"*Dawai!*" In time, the rest breaks also grew unpleasant to us, because on such occasions the guards or other needy Russians simply stripped us of usable boots or other pieces of clothing. They took everything that appeared to be worthwhile, and they were pleased when the man continued to march, either hardly or half-dressed.

On the way I saw one Ivan show his spoils to another, and they made an exchange. More than one of them had collected a cap-full of watches, rings, brooches, chains, etc. One called for a watchmaker from our ranks, saying that he would be well rewarded for his help. The hesitant volunteer was instructed to make two small alarm clocks from one modern one. It required great effort and much time to make it clear that the demand was impossible. Another one was playing with an elegant travel alarm clock, which suddenly began to buzz. It took him only a matter of seconds to throw the devil machine to the ground, as if it were red hot, and to empty his machine gun on it.

On a village street some highly ranked men in uniform are trying their hands at riding a bicycle. A German woman has to give it a test run, and then explain what she did. Their expressions are all baffled — these *Niemniez*[91] have some strange things.

We move to an estate in Pomerania [Pomorskie].[92] In the delousing, which later was frequent and hated by all of us, I experience Eastern culture for the first time. The clothes for delousing were put in a transportable boiler, which was also supposed to provide hot water for washing. During that time, we were completely free of all vermin, but the Russians had this type of hygienic operation running constantly at numerous places anyway.

The machines steam in the yard; then the patient has to walk stark naked to a far-away room in order to wash. There are sufficiently large basins there, or wooden buckets, along with soap and towels to dry off with. Women who are working under the supervision of a Russian medical orderly attend to the operation. We happily scrub ourselves there as long as possible, but then the torture begins, for then we are driven into the cold. We wait for our rags

---

91. The Russian word for German is *Nemets*.
92. An area west of East Prussia. See the map on p. 42.

without any clothes at all. At best, they will be ready in an hour, and then they will be distributed hot and steamed.

We stand for a while on the cold cement floor, on stones, or on the ground outside. Everyone is at the mercy of the weather, and after a short time we conclude (and not without good reason) that hell must be a sanatorium.[93] Only the most iron of natures could hope to overcome such harassment without a severe breakdown.

As we went through the Pomeranian city of Lauenburg [Lebork], the fires there were still burning. It was the same scene in the city of Bütow [Bytow], where as usual Ivan was causing trouble. Before he settles in he throws all the furniture out the window — the beds, linens, carpets, pictures, chairs, etc. And before he does that he smashes it all to little pieces. The beds are always slashed open because treasures could be hidden inside — the feathers lie everywhere like fresh snow. Only then do the occupiers make themselves comfortable.

In contrast to the country, victims' bodies have been removed from the cities. Perhaps they've only been cleared from the streets, but the scene left behind by the blood- and plunder-thirsty hordes remains gruesome as always. And in attempt to obliterate all traces of the brutality, fires were set wherever the atrocities were too great.

We are forced into government offices that remained undamaged, and come across a larger number of POWs who are assembled here. We hear from them that everyone will be transported to the huge assembly camp of H., where there is supposed to be room for about fifty thousand men. A type of military classification is created here, and by means of lists, groups are assembled consisting of 150 men each. It also appears that the food rations are supposed to be distributed on a regular basis, and that the military orderlies and the doctors even seem to be interested in the sick and the wounded.

Seasoned from experience, I step up to a Russian officer without a moment's hesitation. I explain to him that I have stomach trouble, and at the same time I show him my leg, which has begun

93. This is probably referring to the sanitizing process described, not a convalescent hospital.

to fester and swell severely. He inspects me quickly, beckons to a medical orderly, and gives him instructions. Then I am led into a fine apartment, where I am examined by a doctor, and then escorted into the kitchen of a still partly furnished six-bedroom apartment. Two soldiers are lying there. They have been suffering from dysentery for a few days now, and I am the third one to join the group.

The Russian medical orderly first takes me for the customary delousing, which this time, thanks to his help, is completed within a few minutes. Then this gem of an Ivan makes a bed for me in the kitchen, almost as a mother would make the bed for her son. It is a good mattress, placed on the tiled floor with several silk quilts as the underlay, and for covers he hauls in two down feather quilts; I am very, very happy with this change of circumstances. At the foot of the bed there's the bucket with a cover, like the ones the other two patients have.

He soon reappears with a dish of good, fatty soup, along with some bread, butter, marmalade, crackers, etc. My eyes pop wide open at such treasures, but apparently my neighbors aren't especially interested in them. In any case I gorge myself until I'm properly full, and then in an extremely short time I make a very unpleasant mess — in the bucket.

I believed that I must be dying. Everything came out as if someone had turned on the water faucet. The feces were a bloody, foamy slime. During that stay the gallant Ivan never got tired of bringing in the most beautiful things, and then taking them back again, always untouched. In the future, drops of opium, disgusting, bitter pills, and dry porridge oats remained the only form of nourishment. A burning thirst tormented me without interruption, and with all the will in the world I couldn't make myself think of sleep. My stomach constantly had the urge to empty itself.

In the meantime the doctor came in. He looked at me and the bloody mess, shook his head soberly, offered us cigarettes, and disappeared again. After a few days, it took gathering up all of my energy just to reach the bucket on time. The feeling in my stomach was indescribable, followed by the sensation that I was losing my intestines.

The soldiers had long since moved off. We, too, are suddenly loaded onto a LKW, and then subsequently unloaded in the familiar city of L. at a former hotel (due to overcrowding, a military hospital there wouldn't admit us). First comes the customary delousing, and then we are carried to the third floor of the house. We find a spot there in a cleared-out double room. Again we are on thick, soft undersheets, next to ten other soldiers who are lying here because of different illnesses or wounds. Otherwise the house is completely filled with German civilians of both sexes, who for the most part have typhoid fever and die off quickly. Whoever gets sick outside is brought in here because the Russians are afraid of getting infected.

A German nursing staff, mostly women, works under Russian supervision. Medicines and dressing materials are all plundered from the Germans. We soldiers are given preferential treatment, and they watch over us carefully. The Russian medical staff is good here as well, and the doctors look after every single one of us. The food is regular and nourishing, and I begin to chew on dry, rock-hard bread crusts and am able to keep that in my stomach. In addition I get some type of gruel and a few medicines. Finally I am able to find the deep, and long-missed sleep.

I continued to refuse the liquids, and there is no more blood in my feces. But it was high time, for at this point the scale showed 49 kg.[94] With the help of another man I was finally able to use the wall to get on my feet again — then I could stand alone, though like a baby.

Our female nursing staff had either gone through hell earlier, or they were still in the midst of it now. The Red Cross armband didn't in any way protect them from acts of violence, and they could only thank the fact that there were quarantines here, or rather that signs warning of typhoid were put up (the Russians had respect for these signs) — otherwise the Russians would have continued to drag them off to orgies.

We heard the same things over and over again. One brutal act could distinguish itself only in its variation from another. Sadism and perversion were coupled in an inconceivable way. It is impossible, in my opinion, for women who have experienced these types of "human beings" ever again to find their way back to a civilized,

94. This 108 lbs was covering Thiel's 6 foot 4 inch frame.

humane society. But I assume that Russia was intelligent enough to silence forever such women still living at that time.

One day at the crack of dawn there's a lot of commotion, along with some wild shots. Is it May Day celebrations again? Or is it Papa Stalin's birthday? What is told to us seems unbelievable: they are celebrating an armistice. The war is supposed to be over. Hitler is dead,[95] and Germany is shattered. We are just as indifferent to one as to the other. If we could only get ourselves ready for transport as soon as possible, then we could go home. Plans are made, discussed, and then discarded. A huge question mark hangs over everything and everyone.

Today, it is interesting to remember being with those dozen men who came from all classes of our society, and who judged their own circumstances as well as that of other peoples, without being influenced by anything else. No one mourned for Hitler. That Germany was shattered was indeed unfortunate, but it was the natural consequence. In all that had happened, it was not the German soldier, the worker, the citizen, the business owner, nor the scientist who had failed. It was the commanding military officers and the diplomats who had failed. It was they who had not understood early enough and recognized the criminal in Hitler. It was they who did not search for a timely agreement with America and England.

One hopes that the largest part of our country will be occupied by the troops from overseas, for it is impossible that they can be at the same level of civilization as the Russians. Everyone understood that America and England wanted to do everything possible to crush Hitlerism. Many years before, we, too, had come to the realization that the system was grasping for the throne of God, and a world ruled by Nazism couldn't be a happy one. It had probably been necessary to work with Communists in the process, but now the Bolshevist had to be crushed just as much as the Nazi. He will bring the world to another downfall, and the chaos we have experienced until now will seem only the smallest part of that chaos. Even the no-nonsense dockworker from Danzig, who since 1918 has been a registered member of the Communist Party, is of the same opinion.

95. Hitler killed himself on April 30, 1945, and May 8 was V-E day.

The Russians announce through our building that we wounded and sick will be free in a few days. We'll get our discharge papers and we'll be distributed among our home-towns by group transports. Naturally everyone declares himself well enough to leave.

I receive escort papers for a group of nine men, along with instructions to take my time in reaching the city of S[chneidemühl?; Pila?]. There I should report to the headquarters so that we can be put on the train. On the way through the city, everyone is falling over each other, and then we run out of strength. We spend the night at the nearest plundered farm.

The next day we slowly drag ourselves forward, and again, like the day before, we allow ourselves an early rest. In this way we beat all marching records, that is, in six days we arrive at the city of S[chneidemühl]., having managed five kilometers a day.

We found plenty of provisions in the cellars of the farmhouses. We needed only to search in certain places under the wreckage, where we found an ample amount of "overlooked" food. The filthy stove was cleaned, and soon the pots and pans were bubbling. Yet without fail, as we reached for the first bite, Russian rifle barrels set their sights on us through the doors and windows (every rising smoke column alarmed the people in the area).

Hands up! We were searched for any weapons, and then, when I produced my dispatch note, their expressions were not unfriendly. In some cases the guys even allowed themselves to stop and chat, generously distributing their tobacco. A soldier's uniform by itself, even if it only covered half a body, was enough to send the Russians into panic. Then we had peace again, free to stuff ourselves and indulge in some good long sunbathing.

Ivan assembled enormous herds of cattle on the farms, either to slaughter or to take somewhere else. Shrewd Polish-speaking individuals bargained for the best heads with vodka and jewelry, and then drove the cattle into remote strips of forest. They also (secretly, to be on the safe side) took everything from the farms that could still be used. We could not have guessed that these vultures would become our masters of tomorrow.

IV
The Polish Masters

In S[chneidemühl]. I report to the headquarters and, for lack of suitable accommodations, my men and I are kept for three days and nights in the cellar of a briquette factory. Apparently not all of the transport has arrived, but it is supposed to be assembled here and then leave to go *na Odra*[96] (across the Oder). After we have made enough noise, an extremely annoyed guard appears and gets us something to eat.

When we were taken out and brought to the train station, we must have looked as black as the devil. About 120 fellow-captives fill the four cattle cars hitched to an empty freight train, and then we begin to roll. The escort party is reasonable and even generous in distributing bread. The guys give us tobacco as well if we German soldiers sing without stopping. Again, Ivan shows his weak spot for music and song.

At the old railroad junction B[romberg; Bydgoszcz]., which is familiar to us, there is a long conference between our transport leaders and the local department heads, who are wearing brand-new foreign uniforms. We think about it and are able to determine that these men are Poles. Ivan is no longer anywhere in sight. We are moved onto a dead track. Heavily armed men in uniforms order us to exit the cars and march off. I attempt to use my Russian discharge papers as identification for myself and my small group; they are torn to shreds and scattered on the ground. It wasn't until later that we understood

96. "to the Oder," the river running along the border between Germany and Poland, emptying into the Baltic sea. See the map of post-war German Administrative Divisions on p. 107.

The Allied sectors of post-war Germany (1947). Thiel spent his last days of imprisonment at Erfurt, Weimar, and Gotha. He escaped from East Germany (Thüringen) to West Germany (Hessen) by hopping a train from Vacha to Philippsthal. He lived his last years in Kassel. From a map of the administrative divisions of post-war Germany prepared for the Department of State (1947).

the Poles had either stolen us outright from the Russians, or "bought" us for a couple liters of vodka. At any rate, we were in Polish hands.

At that time, the Polish militia were dressed in German SA or SS uniforms. Only the four-cornered hats were originally Polish in their style.[97] Both then and later, these troops were always distinguished by extremely loud commotion and a lot of screaming. They went around with our old 98 rifles[98]; as if they were carrying around pitchforks. But it seemed that there was ammunition by the ton — shots were fired off whether the occasion warranted it or not, just as it was with Ivan. Deceit, cowardliness, and brutality are written all over the faces of this rabble. It seems that the worst is ahead, if the Russians don't show up soon and help.

These were exactly the kind of men whom we saw in our country during the revolution days of 1918; men without any trace of discipline or upbringing — the rejects, the scum of the earth.

Along with Russian military, a comparatively large civilian population filled the streets of the partially destroyed town of B[romberg]. They appear to be neither friendly nor hostile towards us, yet it seems that they are running to their homes to get away from our train. The German street signs, advertisements and firm names are either shattered or replaced by provisional Polish ones. The Russians are obviously "The masters of the house," whereas nominally, the management has passed on to the Poles. We are taken to the refugee camp K[altwasser],[99] a former German work camp, four kilometers from the city.

It has grown warmer — the bare cement floor is no longer disturbing. Here we are permitted to roam freely among the three buildings. They lie outside the actual camp but are secured by barbed wire two and a half meters high. No one has any thoughts of escape — our physical state is much too bad for that. We have to take paper and wood-wool[100] from the other buildings to use as pads for

97. Polish officers' hats were traditionally four-cornered.
98. The 98 model Mauser rifle, the *Gewehr* 98, originally made in 1898.
99. A subcamp that became notorious for the mass killings of the Germans by the Poles after the war. See note 102 on page 110.
100. Wood shavings often used for packing.

sleeping; the last remnants of bread are quickly distributed among us and eaten. Then we go to sleep.

After a few hours, "wake-up" is delivered in the Polish manner, a form entirely new to us. A horde of militiamen storm into the room carrying flashlights and roaring loudly. First they use sticks, billy clubs, the ends of cables and feet to beat senselessly and indiscriminately those lying or standing closest. Everyone has to line up outside and — Hands high! — allow himself to be thoroughly frisked, while another group of brave men ransacks the baggage inside. Again and again a banknote or some other valuable is actually found, and the filthy, unshaven, criminal face lights up under the new square cap.

"*Kolera Niemniez,* " "*Juppt foie motz,*" "*Kurvie sinn.*" I am spelling these phrases incorrectly — at that time they were new to us, but later we heard them every day. They mean: "Damned German," "Your mother's a whore," and "Son of a bitch," and are a key part of the Polish vocabulary.[101]

Then our quarters are cleaned thoroughly. That means that all of the paper and wood-wool we had taken is carefully returned while we are kicked and hit again. The bare cement floor is good enough for the "*Kurvie sinn.*" Then, with a long list of impractical commands and orders concerning camp discipline, threatening the most horrible of punishment in the event of any violation, the horde leaves its place of work.

The next morning we line up to eat. Very few people have any utensils or bowls. Those who don't have any, go along anyway, and, as always in such cases, use the quickly emptied bowls of the men before them. The kitchen is in the main camp a good distance away, and only a short line of civilian prisoners remains when we arrive. We have the opportunity to see a supervisor there who inspects us with great astonishment. He runs towards us and apparently wants to say something. He raises his arms and then collapses. Those standing closest rush to help him but are forced aside by the militia,

101. His definitions are correct: *Cholera* is one of the most common Polish swear words. *Niemiec* is a common word for German. The next phrase is originally a Russian term: *iob tvoiu mat* (here in a Polish form), and the last, spelled correctly in Polish, is *skurwysyn*. Thiel's Polish misspellings have not been corrected.

who draw their guns. Strong kicks keep the man from getting back to his feet, and finally he is dragged into the closest barracks. To our astonishment, he was wearing the tunic of a German officer; his epaulets, almost totally shredded, signified a very high rank. He had probably completely worn himself out here in the camp.

The paths and the square here are strikingly clean and well-swept between the barracks, which appear almost as if they are unoccupied. Just as strange are the numerous figures that can be seen through the windows and doors; they are armed to the teeth, their uniforms weighed down with billy clubs. We didn't know then that we were in one of the most infamous death camps in Poland. Before our arrival, it was there that the greater part of the remaining Bromberg population, among others, had met a cruel end and were buried in the mass graves of the surrounding forest. Since then, the lust for blood has been curbed by orders from above, or the executioners have grown tired. Later, behind the bars and barbed wire, we learn about the camp; reports survived of trucks arriving and departing with machine-gun shots in the night. We heard, too, about other methods, such as dousing the unfortunate with gasoline and burning them after they were made to dig their own mass-grave.[102]

They are serving the last people in the row in front of us. An older man flies down the steps and out of the kitchen barracks; he is greeted with clubs by the militia posted outside. He loses his mess tin and a woman in line picks it up. She, too, is immediately assaulted by heavy blows; blood pours from her mouth and her nose. Driven by kicks, she finally manages to drag herself to the entrance of the closest barracks. The man remains on the ground streaming with blood; then several men are assigned to carry him away.

This is the first time we have experienced such treatment in a prison camp, and naturally we are anything but calm. During the scene, however, other militiamen made a point of taking positions on either side of our column, standing ready to fire. We realize that

---

102. Corroboration (as well as more discussion) of the life in Kaltwasser and other camps can be found most notably in *Dokumentation der Vertreibung der Deutschen aus Ost-Mitteleuropa* edited by Theodor Schieder, and *Schattenjahre in Potulitz 1945* by Hugo Rasmus. Both of these texts were published after Thiel wrote his memoir.

any act of defiance is senseless and would be the equivalent of suicide. Yet, were we not soldiers? Should we have allowed that? The decline of our physical strength was closely related to our loss of spirit.

There was a half a liter of food per person, and for the life of us we could not determine whether what we got was coffee, tea, or soup. It didn't seem that the lukewarm substance had been made for either eating or drinking. A couple of solid chunks that proved to be the skins of mangel-wurzel were swimming around at the bottom of the bowl. Everyone was certain of the diagnosis: our friendly host had poured a sack of dry potato slivers, turnip slivers, etc. (this is something the farmer could buy cheaply to stretch out his animal fodder) into the six-hundred liter kettle. Water was warmed up and then that mixture, without any salt at all, was passed off as the daily rations. Those who "stood out"[103] in some way forfeited their rations, and there wasn't any bread at all. Because of the tight surveillance, no one dared pour out the muck on the way. That was taken care of in the latrine in the barracks.

Another "calm night" follows, along with the same soup as the day before, and no bread. Hunger is a terrible torment. But at midday is "line up for departure." Again there is an extremely thorough "frisking," but we finally get started. Under the surveillance of men on bicycles, we drag ourselves past the town and to the camp of L[angenau; Legnowo]., which is situated ten kilometers to the east. Above the entrance is a huge white and red flag[104]; at the foot of the pole in mosaic is the Polish eagle painted in white.

We stop at the administration. Everyone is registered and put on file, and then we all go into an administrative barracks where we are arranged into groups of twenty men each. I stick with the last group and I, too, pass through the ominous door. We are received by a group of militiamen working hard under the command of some superior. A washroom with about thirty faucets is supposed to clean off the dirt from the trip. We get undressed quickly and lay our things in a pile, and while we are washing, the corporal and his men

---

103. This phrase, *aufgefallen zu sein*, is commonly used by Thiel to identify those who get in trouble.
104. The Polish national flag.

do a very good job — that is, not a stitch of clothing goes unin-
spected, not a shoe-sole goes unchecked — they find simply everything. In this way we lose all that we have, except for a blanket, a
cap, a suit, or rather a uniform, and a shirt. They also took my wallet with the last small pictures of my wife and children.

Hands high! Mouth open! Anal inspection — something could
still be hidden there. This gang of thieves even searches our hair for
any valuables. The corporal pulls me to the side, looks more closely
at two of the pictures in which my children are standing with a
group of German officers, and says:

"You an officer?"

"No!"

"Tell the truth. Nothing will happen to you. You will be put in
another section and meet different comrades there. You will also
have different rations and won't have to work."

"Very kind of you to offer, but I am only a soldier!"

"As you like, but you're not telling me the truth — and why
does your leg look so bad?"

I don't answer. Then he gives an order that I don't understand
and allows me, unlike my comrades, to take my time in getting
dressed. He speaks to me again in good German and says that I am
being taken to the infirmary immediately where there is a good doctor. I recognize the good heart behind a less than pleasant exterior,
and ask him to return the photos, which certainly couldn't have any
value to him. He struggles with it for a moment, and then finally
promises that they will be returned by the administration in the next
few days (unfortunately, I saw them again).[105] As a result of that
exchange I grow bolder and ask the "commander" — which he actually was — for bread or some other kind of rations because we haven't
had anything in our stomachs for days.

"*Kolera kurvie sinn*[106] — stay here! Wait!" The last of my comrades were listening to the conversation with the commander, and

---

105. It is possible that this statement is a typographical error, and Thiel meant to include
"never." It is also very possible that he saw the pictures again and they were mutilated. Or perhaps in such an environment, nostalgia only increases the suffering. In any case, he does not mention the photos again.

106. "You damned son of a bitch." See the Glossary, p. 176.

they also are waiting. A uniformed man appears with a servant who is carrying a basket with pieces of bread. With burning hunger, we quickly distribute them among ourselves and devour them.

I go to the infirmary, where a competent medical orderly gets to work immediately. He is a German soldier, a medical student, who opened up a laboratory connected to the infirmary and works under the direction of a Polish doctor. At any rate, there are still some bandages and medicines, and more are supposed to be coming in. At the instructions of the commander, I receive the one empty bed of the six there. This calm operation is much different from what I've seen thus far.

With its almost eight hundred people from all levels of society, the camp is rather small — we number about two hundred soldiers and eight officers. The rations here don't fill you up, but do keep you from starving to death. In the morning we get coffee with 250 to 300 grams of bread. For lunch we are given a liter of soup with varied amounts of potatoes or trimmings of horsemeat. In the evening, everyone can, if he wants, get a quarter to a half liter of coffee.

Every morning we line up for roll-call. Then, in groups of varying sizes, some people leave for the day to work — either in the camp, or at farms or other businesses outside the camp. In the evening we line up for roll-call again. The "rounds" are made through the rooms, the number of occupants is reported, the doors of the barracks are locked up, and with them closes the day. During the course of the night, the guards patrolling outside communicate by firing off rounds.

We have special privileges in the infirmary and are almost unsupervised. We can even count on receiving preferential treatment from the kitchen, and often the Polish patients, who like to be treated here, reward the services with a handful of tobacco; so we live very well.

The commander is a frequent guest — everyone calls him the "SA man" because he is especially proud of an SA knife that he never takes off. When he is sober, which is seldom, he happily condescends to have a chat with me and goes into raptures about his time as a German soldier.[107] Apparently I'm very much in his good graces,

107. Apparently a Pole, this commander must have been a member of the German army at an earlier time. Thiel does not explain.

113

and I'm able to obtain some privileges for others who had somehow "stood out" at some point.

An unpleasant weakness of his was regularly rearranging the men from one barracks to another, and it made no difference whether it was day or night. It also seemed that he was greatly amused by running the men across the courtyard, individually or as a group, until they could no longer go any further. Hands entwined around the nape of the neck, knees bent — and then hop forward until collapse. Or, the same exercise while one had to hold onto the heels of the other, or up-down, up-down until complete exhaustion — this was a favorite if there were the right water puddles. He enjoyed exercising the women best of all. Nevertheless, no atrocities occurred here.

Two escaped soldiers had some bad luck and were caught; they were very badly beaten and had only their iron natures to thank for their lives. There were plenty of escape opportunities for those who could run. There weren't as many checks outside the camp then, and the Oder-Neisse border had very little security.[108] The majority of the brave men who made attempts were successful, and I cursed my badly festering leg.

With the increase of illnesses, the stock of bandage materials, disinfectants, and medicines was running out by the day. Nothing was replenished. The lice and bug plague increased at the same rate that the food rations decreased. The water supply was very low; there wasn't any soap, and with the rising heat, the number of rats multiplied.

It could no longer be denied or kept secret: the first deaths from typhoid fever occur. The repeated diagnosis, however, is always the same: a weak heart. But the disease runs its course very quickly — with headaches, fevers lasting varying amounts of time, and then painless sleep. The teeth of the dead have the tell-tale black coloring. The two gravediggers have a great deal to do. Separate sick rooms were established for men and women some time ago, with an additional barracks outside of the camp allocated for quarantine.

---

108. After the war, the Allies agreed to transfer all previously German territory east of the Oder and Neisse Rivers to Poland and the USSR.

Every corner is occupied by a sick person. The food rations of those who no longer have an appetite, or of the dead who can no longer eat and whom we always report a half-day later, are welcome supplementary rations for those of us who are healthy.

I am put into another room and am placed "in charge" of several other sick-rooms as well as my own. Among the cleaning women, there is one with whom it is worthwhile to talk; she has good spirits and won't let anything depress her. She is a Baltic German "Countess of B." — she owned an enormous amount of land there, which it seems she has expertly kept in her firm, slender hands, and she ended up here in a rather bizarre way. She is fighting a difficult battle with the lice and bed bugs, and in addition, she is looking after two old men from Riga.[109] One is a pastor and one is a lawyer; they are old friends and stick closely together. They die, one shortly after the other. A few weeks later, the kind countess was eaten away by lice and typhoid fever. She would not be able to show me her estates.

Temporary delousing facilities were running every day and did a pretty good job of cleaning clothes and blankets. But the day after things were cleaned, everything was teeming full of bugs just as they were before. The women suffered the most from this plague. I saw one instance where the hair-clippers couldn't cut some especially badly lice-ridden hair because, for about the length of a finger, a sticky mass congealed in the hair like in a honeycomb. Naturally, no one had a comb or a brush — those were just as scarce as soap — and in the long term, there really wasn't anything you could do with scouring powder and the small amount of water. In desperation, I allowed every patient "to squash" three times every hour, just so that we would not be eaten alive by the filthy things. And whoever was sensitive to the bed bugs — unfortunately I was — was permitted to spend the night on or under the tables because there you weren't bitten as much.

Every day all day we are busy fighting against the tiring nonsense of the camp administration, the gnawing hunger, the lice,

109. The capital of Latvia.

115

fleas, bed bugs, while we try to care for wounds that just won't heal. We increase our own things with those from the dead, who are buried dressed as they were when God made them. Or, whenever possible, we trade their possessions for bread with people outside. Shirts are washed and used for bandages. Every three to five days, the bandages are replaced with paper bandages. There is hardly any cleaning powder for the wounds anymore, and the disinfectants barely sterilize the water. Paper makes air-tight seals around the wounds, and the skin, or rather the wound under the paper, is the favorite playground of lice — it produces an unparalleled itching sensation. Those with the bad luck to be covered by bandages are able to delight themselves and others with all the "scents of India." In addition, the maggots develop with alarming speed and provide all the torments of hell. Thus tortured, the men are beside themselves whimpering day and night, until weakness and death deliver them.

I saw bodies being carried that left a trail of maggots on the path from the contaminated, putrefied camp to the gate, making it look as if cracked buckets were leaking. Always the same diagnosis: weak heart! If the administration was informed of it, I then made a cross and a strike-through on my list. The administration did the same; the kitchen was quickly notified, and the case was settled. None of the relatives received any news, unless one of the eyewitnesses happened to make it home and remembered the addresses. Later, small wooden plaques with consecutive numbers were assigned to the dead — probably to give the impression or prove that in Poland, they did enter the *Niemzi* into records.

On July 19th, I suddenly am no longer able to perform my few daily duties. A leaden fatigue paralyzed my limbs. I see the doctor, the medical orderly, and the familiar nurse at my camp as if through a heavy veil. A dreamlike state followed, one more beautiful and carefree than I had ever experienced. I was a child, peacefully playing with other children, in an unfamiliar countryside that was glowing with sun, in meadows and cool forests. We romp about in shallow streams with all the creatures, tame and friendly.

After four days, I find myself in the midst of strange surroundings again; my head is dull and heavy. They have brought me into quarantine, into the death barracks, from which no one has ever come out living. I am covered with a tunic and my shoes are off— I react immediately to the loss of this treasure. They are nowhere to be seen. I hope they are still in the camp — the efficient grave-robbers are going to be in for it! I also immediately miss my small backpack with clothes, soap, towel, razor, etc. Most likely, they are already divided up.

Damned fly-vermin here — they land on me in clouds, and even more of them on my head. I can't fend them off for the life of me. I must be paralyzed. And what a horrible stench in this damned room — like decaying corpses. My only chance is to get out of this mass grave, but every attempt to move a limb comes to nothing. Only my head raises a little and recognizes the nurse sleeping at a small table. Nurse L.! Yes, she is moving. Other than my cry, the only thing she had ever heard here was the grass growing. She shoots over to me, her eyes wide open like a mother who has just found her lost child. First, she takes a wet cloth and wipes the fly-specks from all the openings on my face, and in the process she tells me what's happening.

No one had thought that I would make it through. She was the only one to give me a chance because supposedly I always had the most energy (the doctor told me later that she never grew weary of wiping the flies from my face). It is too bad that I have never heard anything from the good nurse L., who in civilian life answered to the beautiful name Eleonore von H. She, too, ended up here because of twisted circumstances. In any case, the fact was: death didn't want me this time either.

Because of the large meals, I tolerated another few days of this sanatorium. The bed bugs bit less frequently here, so I could find plenty of sleep. The death barracks was located in a deep, wet depression, and in the continuous rain it seemed like a boat in a pond. Thus, it could only be reached by crossing a footbridge. The water drew me like a magnet because during the past days I commit-ted all of my bodily urges to my pants. Something definitely had to be done with me. Like a dog, I crawl out of the door to the foot-bridge. There I lose my balance and I bathe, not as I planned, but it all goes better than I feared. With great difficulty, I get my pants off.

My shirt and underwear follow, and then, completely unexpectedly, the medical inspector (under Polish command) turns around the corner. His eyes grow big, and a great row follows. I am fished out of the water, laid on a stretcher, my wet stuff placed on top of me, and off we go. I am lucky — we pass the bunker,[110] which is where, under the rules of the camp, I should be — back into the old barracks. There, too, everyone's eyes grow big — but all of my missing things "happen" to reappear.

Because the typhoid fever prevents almost every contact with the outside world, the camp administration decides to open a bigger quarantine ward outside of camp. It is actually at the main camp L[angenau],[111] which the Russians had confiscated but now want to leave, on a ridge about twenty minutes away by foot. Up there, five barracks are released for us to use, and we move in. They set up an administrative, or rather, surveillance headquarters, a storeroom, a mess area, a kitchen, a stable with two horses for fetching water, etc. The countryside around the area is beautiful. The silver ribbon of the Vistula flows through the wide valley beneath us.

The supervision here is less strict because no one is able to entertain any thoughts of escape. Unfortunately, the rations are even skimpier than below. It's been ages since we've gotten any horsemeat; the soups are clear as water and don't have the slightest taste. The daily ration of one kilogram of bread is supposed to suffice for ten portions, and if the supplies don't work out for us, then the rations have to satisfy eleven, even twelve men. Those who aren't as ill as others have to perform the daily camp duties, and that requires more calories. Every person of either sex who doesn't have a fever and can stand up by himself is assigned to a job outside. The camp administration wants to make *zlotys*,[112] which pour into bottomless pockets. Apart from a few exceptions, these workers are exploited to

---

110. Also referred to as "pill-box" or "hot-box," employed for "solitary confinement."

111. He must mean Langenau here as well. It seems he was at Langenau before but not at the "main" part of the camp, as he says.

112. The Polish monetary unit, the *zloty*. Correct plural is *zlotych*. Thiel did not use any diacriticals.

death, or they give up, learn Polish, and allow themselves to be absorbed into the Polish machinery.

Everyone wants to get healthy as quickly as possible and get sent out. Assignment to the worst position possible is preferable to the existence here, where hunger and death are your permanent neighbors. Luckily, we have fewer bed bugs here. In their place, however, many more lice and fleas make existence torture. As before, bandages and medicines are very rare things. With these rations we continue to grow weaker and fatter — dropsy accompanies the typhoid. In the meantime, a number of other open wounds have appeared in addition to the two I have had. When I lie down and put my legs up on two boards placed at an angle, the extensive swelling subsides a little bit. The doctors, both Polish and German, want to amputate in order to prevent necrosis of the bone, gangrene, or blood-poisoning. But I always reject the friendly suggestion.

Here, too, death finds a plentiful harvest. I am in bed number fifteen in barracks room number five. From here I watch the comings and goings in the other rooms and barracks. In about a week, the gravediggers take a good round eleven men from my room. During their time here, many of these men have sat beside me, asked me to take their home addresses and search out their relatives. Even the toughest of them must have seen that one could only survive with a miracle. A pastor was here for some time, and I once asked him if he could find some suitable words of consolation for these people. He was embarrassed and asked that I not demand impossible things from him. He, too, was happy when a pair of corpses were discovered at daybreak, which I concealed well into the morning, even though the rounds were very early here and we were supposed to report such things (bunker punishment threatened) — all just so that we could receive the dead's portion of the bread-ration, which in turn could be divided among the hungry survivors.

We also hid their paltry belongings (the bunker was threatened for this too), and traded them for bread and a handful of tobacco to men who came from outside for this purpose; they, too, just wanted to live. There was only one solution if you still had the courage to want to live: eat. Grass and weeds were pulled up to thicken and extend the meal. At Christmas time, however, the camp was dissolved. One day, the takeover committee, under the command of an unpleasant guy in a white, physician's coat, makes its rounds through the rooms and has everybody present himself naked. The man looks at them from front and back at a suitable distance and has the list keeper write down some brief remarks.

It is rumored that everyone is now going to camp P[otulitz; Potulice]. where we will be put on the transports going home. At any rate, our frame of mind rises. We are getting out of this plague-ridden hole. It can't get any worse than this. Then one day our trucks begin to roll past streets that once were familiar to us, beyond Bromberg and to P[otulitz]., in a forest about twenty kilometers from B[romberg].

P[otulitz]., a small town in itself, takes us in. Meticulous cleanliness everywhere. We see the first militia lined up in military formation. We are given accommodations on the upper floor of a huge mess building and are supposed to wait for further instructions. Doors and windows stay open and may not be closed under the threat of heavy penalty. The icy coldness chases away all weakness and fatigue. It seems that the kitchen is below us. The Polish officer on duty passes by, and we ask him for something to eat — we are in luck, for shortly after he leaves, a huge vat of steaming, extremely tasty turnip soup appears on the floor. A second follows, and for the life of us we can't finish the third. We consider ourselves very lucky for this change, and therefore happily accept the ice-cold night and the even colder floorboards.

A bell brings the camp to its feet while it is still dark. Another ring, three quarters of an hour later, summons the inmates to the big square where the day's work is assigned. The women stand in rows of ten on one side, and the men do likewise on the other. The camp director[113] quickly goes through the columns with the Polish commandant and notes the unit's strength for the day's work. The groups prepared for dispatch are marched off. The square is emptied in a very short time. About three thousand people are handed over to the *kierowniki*[114] (the Polish works managers, bosses) for the twelve-hour work day.

113. This was the "super capo," one of the prisoners.
114. This is slang. Correct plural is *kierownicy*.

The first day finds us in the delousing facilities, which is followed by a bath. All of the prisoners' things are kept very neat. It is a new, very modern, German building, which was originally built as a relocation camp. The barbers are ordered to remove, without mercy, every tiny hair on our bodies. Even the women lose completely everything. We prisoners of war, however, have a special privilege — they leave the hair on our heads. Everything else is totally shaved. The women and girls look crazed with their bald heads.

Then we are marched to the registry where a form is filled out for everybody, and everyone receives his camp number. Mine is 8293. They carry out the "frisking" here in the same old way, which would make every seasoned mugger green with envy. At the last place, we were in fact able to get ourselves a few things, which are taken away again here and moved "*na deposit.*"[115] I had become the lucky owner of a toothbrush and a half a comb, which probably aroused the envy and attention of even those in uniform. I am called to the corner of the room, and they ask me in which part of the SS I was an officer.

"Nothing happen to you if you tell truth."

"No sirs, I have to disappoint you again. I haven't been afraid yet, and it's certainly not going to start today. Go jump in a lake."

I must have "stood out" because an hour later I am taken again, placed in front of another forum, and bombarded with the same antics.

"You no need to work — you go to be with comrades in other barracks" etc. The damned Kazmarecks[116] didn't have any luck by offering me a cigarette either. I would have loved to clobber them upside the head with the burning, highly-coveted smoke — but my toothbrush and comb are generously returned.

We are supposed to be held in the quarantine barracks for at least twenty days. In the first few hours we get a taste of what it's going to be like here — regulations and threats of punishment are pounded into our heads. In subdivided rooms, in which normally there is space for six to nine people to sleep, more than

---

115. Correct Polish is *na depozyt*, which means "to the depot."
116. Kaczmarek is a common Polish name.

double that many men are packed together. The central heating is out of order. Doors and windows remain open day and night. The beds, on which no one may sit, are without mattresses and sheets; there are three to four stools at a small table. The wood-paneled walls and ceilings have to be kept clear of any drops of water, as do the window panes and the half-glass door. In this small, ice-cold room, fifteen to twenty people stand and breathe, or more accurately, freeze. And, whenever the door or the window is closed for even a brief period, humidity collects somewhere. Every drop of water that is discovered results in the following punishment: for a half a day, the room occupants must stand in formation on the drafty floor while the senior soldier and his deputy, stripped down to the belt, stand in front of the open window with their arms folded in the nape of their necks — until they are "finished." In addition to that, all of the wrongdoers are deprived of half their meal.

Here we are harassed, cured, and trained by the cold. There are no more pests; even the bed bugs are either foreign to this place or frozen. I never knew how much cold a man was capable of enduring.

The food is better and above all things, always on time. In the morning, one-quarter liter of coffee, at midday, one liter of mostly thick, tasty soup (although without meat or fat), and in the evenings we receive 250 grams of bread and another liter of thinner soup. On Sundays, in place of the evening soup we get one quarter liter of coffee or tea. We couldn't fill up from it, but our stomachs had been trained so well that they were satisfied.

No one who lived through these twenty days in the quarantine in P[otulitz]. will ever forget them. Every day, the doctors came by punctually and treated the wounds, but no doubt because of the cold, they could not improve our condition. A transport home is discussed just as often as the future life in the camp, which promised to be anything but pleasant.

For Christmas, an enormous tree was put up in the square, and the entire camp had to participate in the celebration. The old "Silent Night, Holy Night" rose up at the command to sing a Christmas carol. Then a frenzy of screams from the hosts, followed by a flurry of billy-clubs on the heads of those "celebrating." There were a number of serious injuries.[117]

The many different occupational groups are sorted out, organized into individual work groups, and in that way assigned to the many different barracks. Only we POWs were permitted to live together. The barracks are as alike as peas in a pod — the type of lodging and accommodation is the same everywhere. Two-hundred-and-fifty to three-hundred men live in each building and are subdivided into rooms with about thirty men on top of each other. The *barackowie* (barracks-commander)[118] has his small office right next to the entrance, and every room has its senior soldier, who is accountable to that commander.

Meticulous cleanliness is everywhere. Women take care of the cleaning duties while the inmates are at work. Only working people live here — the sick or weak are immediately removed and placed in the so-called sick barracks. There they are served Kettle II, and here we get Kettle I — that is, the worker receives one liter more of better soup each day with an additional two-hundred grams of bread, while Kettle II isn't enough for anyone. Time shows that those who end up at Kettle II cannot be helped anymore; sooner or later they all end up "on the sandhill."[119] The Poles only feed those who do good work for them, and those people get only as much as they need to live. Whoever overexerts himself and wears himself out makes a good impression and receives a little bonus in the form of bread or some remnants of tobacco. Then he is the "model-worker" and plays the slave-driver, for the others have to adapt themselves to his work quota. Naturally, these mostly Polish-speaking guys are not very popular, but they cannot be eliminated because they are thoroughly protected by the Polish overseers.

A similar category — for the most part, the worst one — is the

---

117. This Christmas celebration at Potulitz was also described by the author of document 268 in *Dokumentation der Vertreibung der Deutschen aus Ost-Mitteleuropa* edited by Theodor Schieder. The author said that the prisoners were supposed to sing, but only Polish songs, and when someone started singing the German Christmas carol "Silent Night, Holy Night" (*Stille Nacht, Heilige Nacht*) the singing was broken up. (Band 1, Teil II [1953] p. 603).

118. Correct Polish (a slang term) is *barakowiec*.

119. Other survivors of these camps use the same term, *Sandberg*, to refer to the place the dead were taken.

capos (supervisors who don't work with us), who never know whether they are Poles or Germans. In order to please their employer, they act as informers and exhaust the workers placed under them, more quickly or slowly depending on their character. The armed, supervising militia are ninety-five percent illiterate, and during normal times, they would be described as nothing more than thugs. They derive pleasure from playing an active role in running a sick, emaciated, and defenseless *Niemniez* to the sandhill.

The *kierownik* is the all-powerful leader of his respective occupational branch. His salary rises with the level of his productivity, just as his career is dependent on the ruthless treatment, or rather exploitation of his workers. The commander has less to do with the work production. He, along with a staff of aides, is responsible for discipline in the barracks and the camp.

The *nazellnik*[120] is the general manager, and the entire camp with all its bits and pieces are subordinate to him. The *speziallnie*,[121] however, commanded a special department, the political one. It is comparable to the former German Gestapo and the Russian GPU,[122] and everyone is terrified of it. At its time, this specially trained agency drove the Germans to disaster; today it is doing the same to all of Eastern Europe, and tomorrow it will probably steer other states as well. But to where?[123]

I let myself be assigned to an occupational group and work at a *majontek*[124] (farm) ten minutes away from the camp. Naturally, because of my lack of strength, work in the true sense of the word was out of the question. Here I was helped by my many years of experience and mastery of the techniques. So despite my health, I was able to stay with the group.

The *kierownik* watched me and probably expected that I would

120. Correct Polish is *naczelnik*, "leader." It can also mean "governor," "head of department," or "chief."

121. *Specjalny* means "special" in Polish (*specjalnie* is an adverb). The "special branch" meant the secret police. The word was frequently abbreviated to "Spec" to refer to those in the department.

122. The Soviet Secret Police.

123. This is one of the few instances where Thiel refers to the time in which he is writing the letter/memoir.

124. Correct Polish is *majątek*.

be a useful, trained adviser or foreman in the foreseeable future. For that reason, he spared me when I folded in the face of arduous jobs.

There were certain tasks that needed to be done after work, and I happily allowed myself to be assigned them because each person was then permitted to "grab" a handful of steamed potatoes from the pig-kitchen.[125] There were also a number of jobs done during lunchtime, for which we received a pass in the camp-kitchen for an additional portion of soup. Over the days and months hung the banner: food. Constant hunger was the driving force behind us, and the Pole was brilliant in manipulating that very fact to get us to work.

Whoever had the opportunity to be assigned to the storehouse came out with pockets full of grain, and, naturally, there was a banquet right then and there — though there couldn't be any informers nearby. With cunning and luck, every once in a while we were able to roast ourselves a stolen turnip or a handful of potatoes in the ashes of a fire or in a forge fire. The animal mangers were very quickly swept bare whenever the animals were fed steamed potatoes, and we were working there. The distinguished swine in the pig stall were regularly served a menu consisting of milk, gruel, left-over meat etc. Now and then a pair of lookouts covered the raiding party, which successfully drove away the creatures from the nourishing pot. No one pitied the deceived beasts — and we never had stomach trouble.

My biggest worry now is my bad leg. The whole thing is ulcerous from my ankle to my knee, and because of the inadequate treatment, it is putrefied and inflamed. Despite the hard work, my pain is enough to drive away sleep. On the second day after it is bandaged, the smell of the pus becomes unbearable. The orderly and the doctor shake their heads. I can't be admitted into the infirmary because I'm not yet carrying my head under my arm — not until the patient is marked unmistakably by death may he see the Polish-Jewish head physician, who then approves or refuses the admission. Whoever goes to the infirmary has — as we say in the camp — bid farewell forever, or he went there with fractures that could be healed, like a skull fracture.

The time for treatment and bandaging is always in the evening

---

125. Where food is cooked for the pigs. For Thiel's description of this place, see the next paragraph.

hours after work. The head physician comes very late as a rule and, frequently, not at all. Because of extensive government connections, he is also in charge of other camps and prisons — a widely feared man. From the German perspective he is a thoroughly hated and dreaded despot, the father of all harassments, the gravedigger of thousands. A sadist in the truest sense, the Pan[126] Doctor Z., named Zitterbaum. It was not easy to get to see this all-powerful being, and impossible for those who didn't work a specific job regularly.

One evening, a fearless nurse who didn't defer even to this sadist, grabs me under the arm and, contrary to all the regulations, steers me straight up to his desk. "*Co to jest Pannie?*" "What is this?"[127] We show him the unbandaged leg.

"POW?"

"Yes."

"Bullet wound?"

"Yes."

(When he wanted to, the man spoke good German.) Then he flings the door open, bellows to the doctors and screams, "to the infirmary immediately, right away!" That is no longer possible this evening, however, because there are too many formalities like delousing certification etc. that must be done before the gates of the sanatorium will open for me. But I will be admitted the following morning.

Polish and German nurses work there under a head nurse, who is Polish. As a result, the Germans do the work and are thoroughly harassed and exploited. The most meticulous order and cleanliness is everywhere. There are even bed-linen and shirts from refugee and housing supplies, and they are changed every eight days. The beds are the iron, white-painted furniture from old German hospitals. The rations are at a level between Kettle I and Kettle II, so the patients are able to live well.

At my request, my ointments and powder are saved for my leg, and cold compresses are made two times daily with nothing but

126. *Pan* is "Mr." or "Gentleman" in Polish, and in Polish, as in German, titles are often added on to others (as in Herr Doktor).

127. Thiel is translating the Polish here, which means "What is this sir?" It should be written, "*Co to jest, Panie?*"

clear water. I soon notice a certain alleviation and a smaller discharge of pus; nevertheless, the healing process does not want to begin. After fourteen days, the doctor's announces that the framework of my skin[128] has been completely destroyed.

"The circulation is blocked and your leg will never completely heal. Get used to the idea that one day it will be amputated." In the meantime, the nurse who did the bandaging also took a look at the situation (she really didn't have anything else to do in this station), and one afternoon she ordered my wound be given a specialized dressing. My leg was thoroughly washed again, and every open place (she counted forty-two) was treated lovingly with silver nitrate and some caustic liquid stuff.

"I know that you will curse me," she says. "But I hope that we'll make some progress with these things."

Yes, I damned her loving treatment afterwards. Those hours following were dreadful. The pain was agonizing and seemed to overcome my strength and judgment. Roasting over an open fire couldn't have been any different. Kept in that state, I would have immediately permitted them to amputate.

During the night, the nurse creeps up secretly with a piece of bread and a cigarette. She also passes me a light. She is happy for not being strangled by a raving madman.

"I knew," she admits, "that an East Prussian ox like you could handle that procedure."

It actually turned out to be a success. I slept a great deal during the following weeks; I gathered my strength and watched my wounds close little by little without any other medical treatment. A small amount more of lunar caustic[129] helped the worst spots, but that was completely tolerable.

In May it is rumored that all sick POWs over forty who can't work will be put on a transport soon and released to their home-

---

128. In medical terminology, *Netzhaut* (the term Thiel uses) can mean either "retina" or "omentum." Not a physician, Thiel was likely unaware of the precise anatomical meaning of the word as he wrote it and was instead using it descriptively, as in *Netz der Haut*, the underlying structure of the skin. His leg, widely and deeply infected, had probably deteriorated to a condition known as cellulitis.

129. silver nitrate, a highly potent antimicrobial ointment.

towns — as long as the towns were in the areas occupied by the Russians. To get on the transport, a questionnaire must be completed so that they can determine that the prisoner was not a party official or a high-ranking military leader, and thus not a war criminal. Those who joined the party after 1934 as well as those who were members of the SA, the NSKK,[130] the DAF,[131] the Waffen SS,[132] etc., were acceptable as long as they didn't hold a high-ranking position. Every POW was summoned by a procurator (Polish judge) to be assessed and admitted. Thus, the charming man appeared at my bed, his secretary carrying a typewriter, and after careful consideration I state truthfully that I had been a member of the NSDAP since 1938. If I conceal everything, I thought, some malicious informer could use it against me later.

Six days after taking down this statement, they read me a warrant for my arrest, according to which I must stand by for Polish jurisdiction. During this period, I am not permitted to leave the camp for any reason, and so on. What is that supposed to mean? At any rate, everything looked bad, and I refrained from making the desperate attempt at escape only because I was unable to run.

Four months after the ominous warrant for my arrest, I am ordered to the administration. There I am brought to a gentleman who introduces himself to me as the lawyer whose duty it is to defend me. The state is bringing a trial against me soon. I am very suspicious and answer his questions with the utmost caution.

"By no means," he stresses, "do you have any reason to be worried if they cannot prove you had a special position in the party, or rather, belonged to it before 1934. The whole thing is merely a formality."

Other POWs have the same discussion and the same proceedings to look forward to — a couple of Hungarians who were suspected of being members of the SS because they had been found with the tattooed blood group,[133] and a young Bavarian who stupidly stated that he had been a leader in the *Hitler Jugend*.

130. *Nationalsozialistisches Kraftfahrkorps*, the National Socialist Motor Corps, a motorized branch of the SA.
131. *Deutsche Arbeitsfront*, the German Labor Front, a Nazi replacement for the legitimate trade unions.
132. The combat arm of the SS.
133. Every SS man had his blood type tattooed close to his arm pit. After the war, it was proof that the person had been a member of the SS.

Released from the infirmary, I am no longer permitted to go to my old job because of the warrant for my arrest. Therefore, as a precaution because of my leg, I let the doctor give me a "certificate for sedentary employment" and am transferred to the *macziarnia*.[134] In this department, there are several hundred men, women, and children busy with as many tasks as possible. They manufacture straw shoes, bags, mats, hats, and other junk that is then put on sale. Affiliated with the department is the *kosczikarnia*,[135] a wicker work shop in which everything from the smallest sewing basket to sets of furniture are made from wicker. In both departments, the things are produced more or less with enthusiasm.

As everywhere, here, too, one person rushes the other because payment consists of either Kettle I or Kettle II. A very few of the best workers, masters of their crafts, receive an additional 100 to 150 grams of bonus workshop-bread, as reward for the exceptionally quick completion of special tasks.

For a time, I am busy sewing the soles for the straw shoes, and a little later I sew on the upper leather. One needed only to have a somewhat skilled eye and finger strength, capabilities that allowed me to reach the highly sought-after Kettle I in fourteen days. Then I was completely satisfied. The *kierownik*, with the build of a boxer and a ruthless slugger, needed workers for the expanding wicker work shop and had the *capo* ask me if I had any desire to go there. No, I didn't. I fulfilled my work quota here without any particular strain, and there the work was much more difficult.

On October 6th, four fellow captives and I are brought by four times that many heavily armed militiamen to the hearing in the city of N[akel; Nakło]., eight kilometers away. Mine is the first case. The auditorium is filled to the brim — the presiding judge — jurors — prosecuting attorney — court clerk — interpreter — lawyers — the press — everything is assembled that befits a big trial. I am directed to the place for the defendant and asked to sit. As is fitting, two

---

134. *Macziarnia*, most likely spelled *maciarnia*, must have been a slang term for this type of department, perhaps deriving from *mata*, which means "mat." See the list of items that follows.

135. Correct Polish is *koszykarnia* (a slang term).

militiamen carrying machine guns take a seat on either side of me. I am tired, but I clench my teeth and prefer to stand.

The defense lawyer encourages me to let the trial unfold without being afraid. Nothing will happen to me. When I am questioned, I should just say what I said before. It was all just a formality.

The personal data is read off. The prosecuting attorney gives his speech [in Polish], none of which, of course, I understand. He talks for a brief period and works himself into a sweat. The impression he has left is obviously a convincing one. After that, the judge examines me via the interpreter. It is clear: no one wants to, or more exactly, no one is permitted to speak or understand a word in German.

Education. Religion. Whether my parents or grandparents are of Polish descent. Occupation before the war and up to the time I went into military service, or rather, up to the time I was taken prisoner. Whether I had employed Polish laborers or office-workers, etc.

The high court adjourns for further deliberation. After half an hour it returns and announces the lengthy results, from which the interpreter conveys the essentials: three years of prison. And the grounds: the court got the impression that I wasn't telling the truth, that a Party-member[136] of my intelligence and level of education without a doubt had a prominent role in the Party — but even if my statements were basically true, then I still need to be punished, for as a member, I had helped to carry out a certain item on Hilter's agenda, which was: the total extermination of the Polish people.

I am then invited to make my closing remarks — I sum up that I am very sorry to be in disagreement with the proceedings, but if I must be judged by a Polish court, then I demand to be tried by a military court. As for my party affiliation, I have to say that I was familiar with much of Hitler's agenda, but I didn't, until just this moment, know about the part calling for the total annihilation of the Polish people. Also, would they immediately settle the question I put to the lawyer and the interpreter as to whether the sentence was going to be calculated from today, or whether the time I had already

136. As Thiel has mentioned before, he had been a member of the NSDAP since 1938, so that he could keep his farm and receive benefits.

spent in Polish hands — one and a half years — would be taken into account. That question remained unanswered, as was the question of whether I was to be shot immediately or taken back to the camp.

In the evening, the small group of those condemned moves through the streets of the town, tired and emaciated. The local population stares intensely but without any signs of hatred — the escort party is already into its free time; thus they are furious and quite capable of killing anyone attempting to flee — we move back to the camp at a fast march.

Watch-towers lined with machine guns tower above the barracks. As always, the searchlights on the towers explore every street and corner during the night. The guards patrol between the towers on the high embankment behind the staggered, three-meter-high barbed wire fence. As usual, the guards note and examine as thoroughly as possible every pocket, pleat, and shoe of each person admitted. P[otulitz]. opens and closes its gates.

The young Bavarian with me received the same sentence. The two Hungarians were acquitted. In the days following, what happened to us is the sensation, and everyone is discussing it. The conversation about a transport becomes heated again, too, but under these circumstances, it would be impossible to get on it. Our old SA man from L[angenau]. becomes the new commandant. He stops me and lets me tell him about the trial.

"*Kolera, kolera*, an awful thing — but I don't think that they will put you away for three years. It's all just an act. But if it's not, then an amnesty will come soon, as always."

Again the days, weeks, and months eat away at my nerves. The job in the wicker work shop (I gave in and went there) is difficult work for my arms and fingers. I have stiff, swollen fingers, joints, and forearms that hurt like hell. The work requirement grows greater and greater every day, the rations more meager. After all, those in charge of the rations want to live as well, and their pockets are no smaller than anyone else's.

All that in addition to the constant feeling of hunger, however, is easier to endure than the nights in P[otulitz]., which are worth describing. The evening roll call at the big square is hated by everyone and avoided in the most clever of ways if at all possible. Its duration depends on the weather or the mood of the person in charge — one quarter to one and a half hours.[137] No matter the weather, we stand with the others from our barracks in exact formation in rows of ten. Motionless, we await the commanding officer or his representative. On the one side, the men, on the other, the women. The "boss" walking along the blocks is accompanied by the *starzie* (the camp director),[138] who takes down the strength of the assembled units as reported by the barracks-commanders. At the end, new decrees are read off in Polish and German, and the longed-for signal to dismiss is given.

If one of the barracks has stood out in some way, or if someone moved in formation, then the usually intoxicated commanding officer detains barracks number so-and-so and exercises them, right then and there in the emptied square, until they are exhausted. The food is served right after roll call, very quickly eaten, and a half hour later, ringing bells and whistles order us to sleep. Ten minutes after that, all the lights are cut off and everyone must be in bed. Also, the barracks-commander has to have walked through his rooms and taken stock of his people again.

Everyone has washed, dried, and placed his mess tin in the right place. The shoes or clogs are lined up with the other ones right to the centimeter, and, according to regulation, the clothes are lined up just as methodically, folded and stacked. It is called *koskie*, that is, "making cubes."[139] The floor is meticulously clean in the remotest corner. And then always the last conversation, the last question in conclusion to the day: what is in store for us tonight?

At best, the dreaded visit takes place in the first few hours, but as a rule it descends upon the overtired sleepers after midnight. As if there is a fire alarm, a uniformed commando unit (four to six men strong) under the leadership of a *speziallnie* breaks into the rooms, has all the inmates lined up and counted, and in ninety out of a hundred cases finds punishable instances of disorder or uncleanliness.

---

137. Because several numbers are typed on top of one another, it is not clear whether the manuscript reads ½ hour or 1½ hours.

138. "Starzie" seems to come from the Polish *starszy*, which means "senior officer."

139. *Kostkd* is the accusative case of the Polish *kostka*, which means cube. Thus here it means "making cubes," as he says.

Things are scattered about the room, often even thrown out the window. Then they yell, go wild — a truly lively party. These ex-slaves turned masters are seldom sober!

We are punished immediately: everyone in the entire room, dressed only in a shirt, is drilled until he passes out in the stone corridor thirty meters long. Frequently these exercises take place outside around the barracks — preferably in the rain, snow, or ice. The searchlights can make the big camp square as bright as day. A two-to-three-hundred-person block of *Niemniez*, which is divided up for better control, is often "softened up" there. In this manner, the sadists work over the women even more thoroughly than us.

Every eighth night, each camp inmate has to go to the bath-house and take a hot shower. This act, which otherwise would have been very welcome, is turned into torture in P[otulitz]. because we have to wait outside in an endless line, in the overcrowded changing room, etc. for half the night, and then when we fall asleep, the usual inspectors make us forfeit the other half of the night.

The medical inspections came on other evenings, and they, too, periodically robbed us of our sleep. The doctor lights up each person's skin very brightly from top to bottom, examining for any skin diseases. The head physician arranges reviews in a certain order, to which he invites prominent figures from the camp administration, and performs them in the following manner: in a room next to the bathhouse — it is dazzling bright — the committee inspects every male and female prisoner more or less intensively from front and back, bottom and top. On this occasion, the barbers receive orders to clip, or rather, shave this or that person's hair that has grown too thick. The interminably long standing is just as unpleasant as the lost night's rest. This production is called "the scabies show." Many women are crying, and the next day there is indignation and rage.

The bed bugs in P[otulitz]. cannot be forgotten. We were at the mercy of these beasts as well. Unfortunately, I was one of the majority who was badly plagued by these creatures. They simply bit us until we awoke, and so began the pointless hunt through the dark. The bites burned like fire; there was even nasty swelling. Sleep was out of the question. Luckily, the filthy creatures disappeared in the winter.

One day, about sixty men and an equal number of women are

called outside and assembled. I am among them. We become uneasy because we see that it is a punishment for someone having done something wrong. What do they have planned for us? But everyone is worn down. We have become so impassive that the sandhill really doesn't seem that disagreeable anymore.

We are put into brand-new grey prison clothes that have a wide red stripe on the left leg and a wide red triangle on the back. We are taken to a remote and very heavily guarded barracks. The women are dressed the same and put next to us. Our new home is called the punishment barracks — we are the kind that needs to be driven especially hard, that must be kept under extra surveillance, that should be finished off quickly. We cannot leave the barracks except to work.

Special jobs are available by the ton. The trucks (beautiful American Dodge trucks maintained by our mechanics) roll up even in the nighttime with loads of wood, coal, and foodstuffs. They need to be loaded and unloaded, and thus our nights are shortened.

The inspection checks are especially quick and rough. Under the thin fatigues, we wear a small linen shirt and the same kind of pants. The clothing is just fine for the tropics, but for the unheated accommodations in P[otulitz]. with the eternally open windows and twenty or more degrees below freezing, it is unsuitable. Whenever we found a newspaper, packing paper, or remnants of them, they were immediately placed on our body or wrapped around our legs, and at night, with varying amounts of success, they were closely guarded against the reach of the inspectors. It must have been obvious to everyone that, in the long run, it would be impossible to endure under such conditions.

Again I must report to the administration, where I am given the bill for legal costs in the amount of 1490 *zlotys*, payment expected immediately. I kept a straight face and remitted to the state my property in East Prussia. (By the way, when I was discussing the verdict I forgot to say that my sentence also included the confiscation of all my possessions and the forfeiture of my civil rights).[140] "*Kolera*

140. An interesting change in tone; this statement leads one to believe that Thiel is writing quickly and fluidly (as one would expect one writes a letter to a brother), and that he does not intend to revise it.

Niemniez, jids na baracki" — that means "Damn German — beat it back to the barracks."[141]

As an excellent worker, I had a "number" near my *kierownik* and therefore couldn't get away from my work-station, not even when men were chosen for the reconstruction of Warsaw, and I was put on the list. For the most part, my other comrades were distributed to the cart-convoys. This activity was a special form of slave-driving. Groups of fifteen people replace the draft animals on a former munitions cart. The human teams drag thick planks, boards for the carpenter's workshop, bricks, sand, and stones back and forth — everything that needs to be moved around a town. The daily quota is huge; the loads are heavy. Four strong horses would have had a hard time with a load of wood being pulled by fifteen women. Two people pulled a cable at each axle. The same at the front of the cart, two on a cable; one person was in the lead, and two were shoving from behind. A *capo* with one or two militiamen make sure that the team always maintains the right speed, and frequently they run into something.

On the *majontek*, the plow horses are spared in the same way, for there the women have to pull the harrows and tractors. The most extreme kind of slavery — like in the age of Nero. The peat bogs, filled with water and ice, are emptied out in the spring by bare-footed women and girls, and that's before the true slave labor begins. The sandhill redeemed most of the tortured and beaten. And no one was permitted to say anything if he didn't want to run the danger of being sent to the bunker for spreading "untrue" rumors.

Near the camp, a sports field was constructed that cost the lives of hundreds. The people came back from work with their backsides, backs, heads, and feet cracked open. They weren't able to stand, lie down, or sit. Many women and many robust men hanged themselves during the night to avoid this torture.

A nurse in the infirmary dropped a thermometer. Result: three days in the bunker, and afterwards, the cart-convoy. Another didn't follow a notice on the board when she was supposed to. Result: three

141. Correct Polish is *Cholera Niemiec, idź na baraki.*

days in that cellar of death, and afterwards, the cart-convoy. Bunker punishments were handed out for the slightest offense. The stay there — in a dark, bare, and cold cement cellar, the inmate completely naked, no food, periodic kicks, fists or billy-clubs — was not exactly popular. Water was provided for cleanliness, but it had to be mopped up repeatedly with a cloth. And if anyone thoughtlessly told of his experiences there, he was quickly locked up again (the informants worked very well). He preferred not to say anything more after that.

I saw naked men who got out of the bunker during the checks, and then run down the camp streets as though the devil himself were behind them. But the pallbearers' stretchers were in constant use — their loads wrapped carefully in blankets. Weak heart! Day by day on schedule, the gravediggers passed by my work station with their burdens. A rather big coffin on a small truck — yes, here everything runs its orderly Christian course — and the men always have to work together to make one arm or another leg fit under the lid. The lid must always close because that's the rule.

Then the load rolls to the sandhill. A hinge must be opened over the pit. The bottom of the box opens up and the load (depending on its size, there are three to five completely naked bodies of either sex) commits itself to the ground, and then is covered up. In P[otulitz]. in 1946, the average number of dead per day, according to irrefutable records, was 6¾ people from a total of five to six thousand inmates.[142]

One time a group of four women "stood out" and was sent to the bunker at the command of the chief physician. This devil in disguise either didn't soften them up enough over the following days (as "doctor," he visited the bunker inmates several times daily, accompanied by specially chosen thugs), or he wanted to use a new way to make them speak. At any rate, he had a bucket placed in the corner with chlorinated lime for the purpose of disinfection, and as time passed it took on water. Thus an unfortunate accident — the poor women were gassed.[143]

142. At this pace, the death rate would be almost fifty percent per year. It is not clear what "irrefutable records" he is citing.

143. The simple addition of water should not release chlorine gas, but perhaps the doctor added something else as well.

Another popular means of assuring order was "placing" the sinner in the middle of the square or at a fence, making him stand motionless in the scorching heat or severe cold for hours, hands clasped in the nape of his neck, until he was carried away. These are a few of the daily images from P[otulitz]., and that was how one lively young man lost all of his toes to the cold and the doctor. The number of broken ribs, knocked-out teeth and bashed jawbones was also considerable in proportion to the number of inmates. Very seldom was there anyone among the civilian internees with healthy eardrums or kidneys that hadn't been kicked in.

At that time, most of the women were already badly swollen and without their periods, mainly because of the insufficient nourishment, but also because of the persistent colds and the extremely great physical demands. The nurses calculated that the greater percentage of the twenty to thirty year-olds would never be able to give birth again. Every day women well-advanced in pregnancy are admitted from outside commands, from both the towns and the country; of course the Russians and the Poles are always "innocent." Ninety-eight percent of the infants live a few days at most. Lack of nourishment. Afterwards, the farmers pick up the women again; refusing to leave is not permitted. Here we go again! Once more the captors' system proves successful. The women were always itching for life outside, and despite any other objectionable aspects, they happily seize the chance that they will have enough to eat.[144]

We happily sneak up to these women or have others pass them our home addresses — written on the smallest shreds of cloth (surveillance is ingeniously strict here as well), which they then sew on to themselves somewhere and take out. Many relatives received the first news of us in this way, and then stupidly went to the post office very happy with correctly addressed letters in response — the letter was opened here; the courier was discovered after the course of the investigation and then severely punished. There were hardly any other way to contact one's relatives. Escapees would never let their intentions be known beforehand, and if they did, then they had their

---

144. It appears that the success ironically described by Thiel here is that since the circumstances in the camp are so intolerable, the women prefer to take the chance of being raped outside the camp in order to get enough to eat.

notebook of addresses in their head. However, the majority of homes at those addresses had long since been destroyed by bombs or emptied by death. A Red Cross commission could have shown its face to the POWs at least once — but we never saw anything from this fine international institution later either.[145]

Christmas 1946 has passed. Holidays are hated even more than Sundays. When we worked through such days, there was no need to make any note of them. But over time, our overseers lost the desire to work on Sundays, and therefore they decided to have us work only to midday, adding the six lost hours to the following week. In addition, they required us to do a number of barracks-duties during the Sunday free time; they reduced the portions of food, and we were forbidden to go for walks — thus these afternoons were only another burden.

On Christmas, P[otulitz]. had two free days. Nothing could be done other than regular barracks room duties. Everything unheated, the floor wet and icy, the soup thin and meager. In the days before, the bread was distributed straight from the oven because there wasn't any flour again.[146] Half the bread ration was distributed on the first day of the holiday; nothing on the second day. We starved, and even worse, we froze. Even the most stalwart of us had forgotten all of the lovely songs. We had Christmas in P[otulitz]., and we didn't forget to wish Poland all the best.

The rheumatic patients have great difficulty dragging themselves through the coming months. My body has ceased to belong to me for a long time now. The punishment barracks was dissolved; we are redistributed to the old barracks. The red markings on our uniforms have lost their meaning. When will there be a discharge transport for the POWs? After a transport in late fall took away several

145. Because the POWs had been distributed among the camps meant for interned civilians, they were outside the authority of the Red Cross and not bound by compliance with the Geneva Convention. However, the Red Cross did attempt to gain access to some of these camps, almost always unsuccessfully.
146. It was not unusual to eat bread on the stale side; it was just dipped in coffee or soup when it got stale, while other bread was baked to be set aside. But now, with flour running out, the Poles are distributing the bread straight from the oven.

hundred sick civilians incapable of working, new rumors circulated that in the spring another transport was supposed to be arranged for us. Will we be permitted to see our homes, wives, children, and relatives again? News leaks out that the victorious western powers were supposed to have demanded that the Russians extradite us. The Polish press, insofar as we are sometimes secretly able to see smuggled-in old newspapers, is full of propaganda and acts as if Poland had won the war without any help.

Every new day makes us more impassive and indifferent. Even the oldest jokes have lost their force. The people become moody and irritable; thus, they make their existence even more difficult for themselves.

On May 3rd I am handed letters from my brother and from my wife in Kassel.[147] The most important and thrilling news is that, except for my young son and a brother, all of the other relatives are living, safe, have a roof over their heads, have plenty to eat, and are waiting for me. On that day, I took control of my weaker self (which was ready to give up) and I commanded it: no matter what happens now, you are going to stick it out.

The next morning the *kierownik* summoned me to his office — on the way there I quickly wondered what I was being blamed for, and whether or not he would hit me. If so, I wouldn't back down. My last reserves of strength should be enough to lay the big-shot on his face. No one has touched me thus far, and no one will and go unpunished.

When he wants to, he speaks good German, but usually he speaks with his fists first. A long line of comrades, women, children, and even the *capos* have felt them and can say a few things about a call *na Büro*.[148] He doesn't send anyone to the bunker; he gets his own justice right then and there, which in some respects appeals to me.

"You have complained of bad treatment here, why?"

"You've been badly served by a pathetic informer who couldn't

---

147. Apparently the ban on correspondence has been lifted. Thiel makes no mention of this change.
148. *na* is Polish for "to." *Büro* is German for office.

have heard me complain personally, but if he reported some criticism of mine, then I can't change that."

"And what is your criticism?"

"You cannot expect someone in my position to be complimentary of you."

"Did you have workers yourself before?"

"Many."

"I want to know whether you yourself have complained about me."

"So far, I've had no reason."

"And what do you think of Poland?"

"I really wouldn't have expected such a question from you; I love my fatherland as much as you do yours."

The examination ended with that. Again I was lucky. He knew before I did that I was leaving P[otulitz]., and before I left, he probably wanted to talk with the *Niemniez* who never avoided him.

On that same afternoon, I am sent marching to an unknown destination. The group consists of the young Bavarian, two farmers and four women, of whom one, a former hotel-owner, had also been sentenced to three years because of party membership.

Two militiamen, pleasant companions, allow themselves and us to take our time in reaching the train station S[lesin]., eight kilometers to the east.[149] The train has already left. We are led to the rural police station there for the night, and the next morning we are supposed to be taken to B[romberg]. on the train. The station is a former schoolhouse, occupied by a half dozen good-natured guards who take us in and treat us like human beings.

The women are immediately sent to the kitchen, and soon an enormous bowl of boiled potatoes is ready for us on the table with coffee. We stuff ourselves, and then both of us soldiers are given cigarettes. A windowless room, bolted securely, becomes our quarters for the night.

The train was more punctual than our guards. We wait until midday and then roll towards the familiar city of B[romberg]. Nothing has changed since we last saw it. Piles of rubble and dirt lie just

149. More accurately, it is about eight kilometers northeast.

as they did almost a year and a half ago, and the all-powerful Russians liven up the townscape exactly as they did before. The population gazes at us with amazement as if to ask: "Is that still going on?" We keep moving, as if in another world.

The police administration building opens its basement door for us. The few cells are occupied mostly by uniformed Poles because of drunkenness; they sit there for a few hours, a day, or even overnight. My young comrade is made to clean the cells and he returns with bread and cigarettes. We have been separated from the others we marched with. Late in the evening, the officer on duty opens the cell door, bringing his morning snack. He offers us cigarettes and talks with us about military things. Everyone in this building is convinced that from here we will be brought *na Odra*. Our sentence is noted with only a shake of the head; no one believes that we will be imprisoned.

At noon the following day, the two of us travel to the train station with double the guards. A train on a narrow gauge railroad takes us to K[onitz; Chojnice]., the end of the line. The police station there hands us over to different guards. They talk with the prison administration on the phone, reload their machine guns, and we continue through the small town. Near the edge of the town there is a huge, ancient church, and behind its main entrance we must stop.[150] A small door in the massive church wall opens. We are standing in a spacious hall that is sealed off on the courtyard side by a single set of wrought-iron bars woven into many more in the church vault.

My first thought: prison. My second thought: peculiar, that prisons almost always stand wall to wall with places of worship. On the right and the left there are old, heavy oak doors standing half opened, covered with wrought iron. There are offices and guardrooms like in a barracks. Clerks and militiamen busily come and go, but instead of the customary weapons, they are carrying several heavy old keys. We are scrutinized with a great deal of curiosity. The old threadbare tunics, the caps, and our composure distinguish us as

---

150. For some reason, Thiel uses the Polish word *stoi* here, which means "someone stands," or "is standing," which obviously means "to stop" or "wait" in this context.

soldiers, and thus we get a number of questions — whether we were POWs, what crimes we had committed, how many years? I act deaf in response to every question addressed in Polish, and my young companion follows my lead.

In the meantime, we are standing wearily, almost fit to drop. We're waiting for the appropriate authority, the commanding officer; he is being fetched from the town. He finally appears in front of us bearing the insignia of a first lieutenant. In faultless German, he asks me where we're from, which court had convicted us, etc.

"That must have been a mistake. But it will be cleared up — I'll call right away."

Then he goes to call, returns, regrets to have to keep us temporarily, and finally instructs a guard to take us away. The man seemed to be agreeable and objective — ostensibly he didn't want to take us at all.

A jailer leads us through the small interconnecting door into the inner courtyard and to the entrance of the actual prison. We stop at the left of the entrance outside another office and in front of another thick set of bars. My companion is called in immediately. Meanwhile, several jailers hanging about try to talk with me in Polish again. And again I don't respond to anything — the faces, filled with hatred, won't let it end at that.

One of the guys runs at me like lightning and tears the cap right off my head. With the pointed end of his boot, he kicks it a little distance away and orders me, in Polish again, to get it. I don't "understand" anything, but grinding my teeth I keep an eye on this hero. The others take an interest in the eagerly anticipated game and spur him on to kick the son of a bitch in the gut. The outcome would have been uncertain if the door hadn't opened and my young comrade hadn't stumbled out with a bright red face.

A "commander" is sitting behind one of the three desks, playing with a billy club, a cigarette in the corner of his mouth. He immediately bellows at me in his language, demanding why I can't go any faster. I don't "understand" him either, and I say that I don't know the Polish language.

"I will teach you Polish in fourteen days with this here," at which he jumps up and holds the club right under my nose. But he doesn't strike because I suddenly ask him, "You are a Polish officer?" He stops short, contemplates. It is apparent that in my question he has become what he would like to be — and then prefers to satisfy himself with loud, wild threats.

"You are a POW? *Kolera Niemniez*— here you are a prisoner, and if you happen to come out alive, then you can be the King of England for all I care. And remember — this is not a jail; this is a penitentiary.[151] You were an officer?"

No answer.

"How many Poles have you murdered?"

No answer.

"We have the means here to break you damned Germans —*na zellie*" (to the cell).[152] Another jailer leads us behind the bars to a stone staircase past the second, third, fourth, and up to the fifth floor, where we are taken by another "floor attendant." He first checks us thoroughly but nicely for weapons. Then, one of the numerous doors opens up and closes again behind us. We are doing time now, literally behind lock and key.

The welcome here was not so good. The commander kicked my young companion in the gut and tried out his billy-club on his shoulders. I can't shake the feeling that even worse lay in store for us, that it will all depend on how well we control our nerves. Three years here? In a cell like this? Defenseless against the caprice of knaves like the ones we were left with downstairs? No and again no — impossible! This building, these quarters might very well be the final stroke, the end. But if so, then with composure. These guys, who throughout their history were never able to feed themselves, who kissed the hem of our garments for receiving only slaps on the wrist after robbing us, as well as for the seasonal work they begged from us — under no circumstance will these guys break me or see me grovel. I succeed in transmitting my resolve to my completely broken-down comrade as well.

The key rattles again. A pair of bolts snap back. In the door

---

151. One is incarcerated in a jail while awaiting trial, or for minor offenses; the penitentiary is for longer sentences and more serious crimes.

152. Correct Polish is *na celę*.

stands a grinning prisoner with a sparkling aluminum kettle in one hand, an equally shiny ladle in the other, the jailer behind him. We have neither spoons nor bowls, but the man brings the missing items as quick as lightning, fills the bowls to the top — bang!— the door slams shut. It seems that everyone here is in a damn hurry.

The soup, over a liter, is not any worse than that in P[otulitz]. We have little appetite, however. The long disturbing day, the strain on the nerves in this sanatorium — we just aren't able to eat it. Again the sound of keys and locks.

"Do you want more?"

"No, we have enough."

"Here is your bread." The prisoner (he is the trusty) passes us two equally cut thick slices while the guard offers us a light. We just look at the man dumbly. Is he trying to find a new way to toy with us? Nevertheless, I search for my second-to-last cigarette and lean forward as if receiving a light from a waiter in a bar, in this case *Pan oddcziaownie* (the jailer for the hall or the section, or commander).[153] In Poland, everyone in uniform answers to "commander."

The prisoner was burning with curiosity and chatted with my comrade while the *Pan* who offered the light asks all the relevant questions. Bang. Again the heavy door slams. We had not experienced this yet; not only can we smoke, but we are even offered *oggien* (a light).[154]

Our living area is five and a half paces long, one and a half paces wide, a small table, one stool, an iron plank bed that can be folded against the wall on iron hooks with a chain. There is a small wash-stand that also serves as a toilet when you remove the basin, a small water pitcher, a small wall cupboard for the bowl and spoon. When you climb up on the stool, you have a view of part of the courtyard through the bars. The walls here are over one and a half meters thick.[155] The floor is made of old, well-trodden but shiny oak boards.

Naturally, sleep on this first night is out of the question, even if we both had space in the bed. A clock tower sounds every quarter

---

153. *Oddziałowiec* is slang for departmental head.
154. Correct Polish is *ogień*, which actually means "fire." But it is slang for "a light."
155. The manuscript reads 1½ meters, but the "1" might be crossed out.

hour, and in between that booming, we here the shouts of guards in the courtyard being relieved. The massive yard walls bristle with glass pieces, and are guarded with machine guns from structures on the roofs.[156] Spotlights scan the walls in short intervals and periodically, as a check, our cell is lit up through the tiny spy-hole in the cell door. We are — without question — behind lock and bolt.

A bell sounds at dawn the first day and brings the building to its feet. Up here we only faintly hear the rising sounds. A quarter hour later comes the same single ring. Then in short intervals come two rings, three rings, four rings, etc. At eight, it is for us, that is, the last ones. The key and bolt rattle. The toilet pails are put outside and at the same time water is received. A half an hour later there is a quarter-liter of coffee and the same amount of bread as in the evening — altogether, about four hundred grams. We are still eating when the door is opened again and we are offered *oggien*. The last cigarette is shared.

Then a new prisoner slips into the cell like greased lightning; he came within a hair of getting his heels jammed in the door. His visiting card is a pair of hair-clippers, and in five minutes our heads are shaved bald. It is futile to attempt to draw the man into a conversation. He remains mute and after a special knock, thrusts himself out of the cell door just as quickly as he entered.

After that, the guard leads us on an intricate route through several corridors and a number of barred gates to a room where we have to hand over all of our personal gear. It is registered and disappears into a sack. A brand new uniform is hurled in my face as at P[otulitz]. My feet end up in new clogs, a new shirt, underwear, a handkerchief, blanket, sheets, pillow case, and bowl. Wooden spoons follow. Back to the cell. Now we have the proper stuff and can't be distinguished from the others in any way.

In the meantime, a pail of water was emptied out in the cell, chlorinated lime added to it, the straw mattress shaken out. We know all about that. We clean it up. We are barely finished when we

---

156. A description of the practice of putting broken glass on top of the walls to prevent people from climbing over them — an inexpensive form of barbed wire.

are taken out and put in another cell, where the same messy routine rules, where we clean up again. We go to a third from there, which is cleaned up just as nicely. After several hours of "duties," we go back to the old cell, find the first scene once again and start over. After the floor is also polished with bottles of cleaner, we get a breather.

Exactly at noon, the bell rings, up to eight rings just as it did in the morning. The sections summoned with each ring charge out during the intervals, that is, the designated units of six to eight equally-spaced men drag themselves across the courtyard and into the kitchen — everything happens on the double — towards the full aluminum kettles. The bars at every hall and stairwell were carefully unlocked and locked by the guards on duty there. It is impossible to talk to any of the other prisoners on the way, and if a word or shout is heard, then it is immediately to the bunker for both parties.

The quality of the food is about the same of that in P[otulitz]. At noon we get one liter of pretty watery, almost clear soup, and in the evening, we get a half liter of the same stuff, the only redeeming qualities of which were that it was always hot, served exactly on time, and was easily digestible. The quality of the bread could be described as good. Exactly an hour after the meal is served, there is the same ringing of the bell *na kubla wodda* (for the water pails).[157] The one or several toilet pails are brought out from the individual units to the courtyard in the same rotation as before, and we line up in formation. The buckets are filled with washing water from the pump there, and are taken back. There is central heating in every cell, but there aren't any flush toilets, or rather, there isn't any plumbing at all.

Dinner is served at five-thirty. At six is *kostka*[158]; we take off our clothes with a roll-call afterwards — everything except our underclothes is arranged exactly in a cube on a stool or a bench in the corridor. The *zellownie* (cell-leader)[159] makes the inspection rounds; groups are announced and counted, and according to the regulations, we are dismissed with a *dobranocz* (goodnight).[160] In contrast to

157. Correct Polish is *kubeł na wodę.*
158. *Kostka* means "cube." Thus, at six they have "cube time," or fold and stack their clothes. See footnote 139 on page 132.
159. Correct Polish is *celowny* (sing.), *celowni* (pl.).
160. Correct Polish is *dobranoc.*

P[otulitz]., there are no more assaults during the night. And if, after the roll-call, the inmates all beat each other to death, the cell door stays closed until morning by regulation.

On the third day we get an addition — a Pole who was sentenced to fifteen years for collaboration with the German occupation authorities. The guy is obviously a plant. We are extremely cautious and don't allow ourselves to be tempted into making any remarks whatsoever. His report was probably a failure because then two more arrive on the scene; they were given ten and twenty years for similar crimes. It is difficult, but we don't let ourselves get tricked by these guys either.

Even though the others don't react to any German words (and we don't want to show that we can understand a little Polish), we discover a great deal about the building that is worth knowing. Of about seven to eight-hundred prisoners, not six percent is German. One-hundred-and-forty men in uniform guard the group. All levels of Polish society are represented. The intelligentsia: priests, lawyers, government officials, officers who are imprisoned because of cooperation with the Germans, possession of firearms, desertion, etc. Numerically this group balances another category, of whom a number are illiterate. They are there from five years to life for the same crimes but also for robbery, murder, and looting. I later got to know many of these interesting and often pleasant companions.

On the fifth day we are brought to the *speziallnie*, who in the meantime has already asked his informers for an opinion of us. After a long absence behind the ominous door, my companion again has the bad luck of coming out with a battered head. He didn't confess to me until the evening that he had been hit in the stomach as well.

Outwardly very calm, I face a smiling, stocky man who immediately asks me in Polish for my military rank. When I apologize that I cannot understand him, he calls for an interpreter. I should admit that I was an SS officer because they had proof of it. How many Poles did I murder or have murdered? The usual antics make no impression; I prefer to remain completely silent. Then the good man pulls out the desk-drawer and lays a Mauser pistol next to a billy club on top of the desk. I am to choose one or the other, and if I don't speak up immediately, he will make the decision himself.

"I cannot prevent you," I answer, "from having me starved or killed in this charming building, but you have no right to treat me this way." He didn't need the interpreter for everything; he spoke a fair German:

"We will talk again." And then in Polish he continued, "By then you will be broken and groveling." At any rate, I was dismissed, and was very happy to have survived the most feared examination in the camp.

On the same day we are moved into another wing for fourteen days of quarantine. The cell, considerably bigger, held seventeen men. Everyone had his own plank bed; they were arranged in two-level bunks as in a barracks. The inmates are taciturn because everyone suspects everyone else of being an informer. No one spoke or understood German for fear of arousing suspicion, and if anyone did, it was whispered secretly. The *zellownie*— as everywhere, a well-chosen blackguard — uses his authority in the most despicable ways possible. Those who oppose him don't get a minute of peace; he informs against them to the *speziallnie*, and then they couldn't dream of a worse hell.

There is no work-requirement except for the daily cleaning duties and the usual punishments, but everyone can volunteer for work outside. In fact, prisoners are the only people working in the prison garden and on the farms. They also do time in the carpenter's shop and a motor mechanic shop. In addition, there is a wicker work shop in operation, for which I, however, show no interest. The jobs outside are in great demand because the days there are varied and pass more quickly. Also, the hated indoor duties are discontinued when you do an outside job. However, then we need calories, which only those who repeatedly received packages could manage, or that is, consume.

For a few weeks I tried out the garden and the field, which resulted in good-looking, brown skin; nevertheless, I quickly lost my strength. So that I wouldn't have to work, I went to the infirmary for treatment by purposely causing an inflammation in a freshly opened leg-wound. In the meantime, I also got to know the local bunker — it was very simple:

My cell lay on the second floor so that through the high bars you could see a part of the small courtyard in which a row of prisoners completed their daily quarter-hour walk. Five paces separated them, one after the other in a circle around the lawn, as stipulated by the regulations. Standing at the window was just as strictly forbidden as looking up from below. I recognize a man in the marching ring whom I knew very well from P[otulitz]., and with whom I frequently and happily spent time there. And now to my great dismay, he appears here. Perhaps my desire at least to nod to my old friend, L., was telepathy — he looks up to me, is just as delightfully surprised but then is so stupid as to wave to me. I hear only a few commands and shortly afterwards the opening of my cell door. Yes, I waved to a man down there. Down into the basement, through endless passageways — we halt in front of one of the numerous doors. I undress completely, and the heavy door slams behind me. I can't see anything, and I'm standing in ice-cold water up to my calves. Three paces long, two wide, bare cold cement beneath my feet and on the walls. A damned nice dwelling, this miserable hole. The next day it is difficult to keep my composure, to keep from falling at the feet of the guard who opens the door, and to put on my clothes without help.

It gets around that a young doctor from P[otulitz]. has been posted in the infirmary here. I knew him from the description, and I definitely wanted to see him. I report for treatment with my open wound, and after taking care of many formalities, I make it in. It is actually he. A pair of scissors falls out of his hand when he recognizes me, and during the examination he orders my immediate admission into the infirmary. The Polish medical orderlies, however, are staunchly against it; a *Niemniez* who obviously knows Doctor K. should not be permitted any bed rest. The doctor indeed has to provide treatment here, but is not to say anything and certainly is not to give any orders. With a flood of Latin expressions — he knew how to handle the guys here too — he butters them up and arranges it so that *jutro* (tomorrow) I am to be presented to the chief physician.

The chief physician, a notorious lush, was extremely drunk the next day as always, but he happily and willingly allowed me to see him, and he ordered my immediate admission. I spent my most wonderful weeks in the prison infirmary. Dr. K. visited several times daily. He always called on me last so that we could smoke stolen cigarettes together. We never ran out of things to discuss, and when the Polish masters complained about our talks, he even had enough backbone to bare his teeth.

In time, we became regarded as comrades from the front who wouldn't give in here either, and to whom one had to show respect. The other patients in the room, altogether eleven, were Poles who regularly received packages from which we, too, were fed. A good trait of the Pole was his good-naturedness and his generosity when he didn't have to fear any trouble, as in this case.

The food in the infirmary is a little bit better than the food before. The majority of the patients ate only half of it, so that here for the first time I had enough bread. Those who were sent tobacco silently rolled one cigarette each for the *Pan* Doctor and the *dobra Niemniez*,[161] who, in the evening, never had to be asked twice to tell stories about adventures or things from books, things that were unfamiliar to most of the people there. And then they sat anxiously on the edge of the bed like children, and couldn't hear enough.

Every day, each patient was given a small quantity of cod-liver oil, which very few drank. I took it, even with great reluctance, but in that way I always had a quarter liter of a rebuilding substance in my body. Plenty of sleep, rest, and food gave me new strength within three weeks. Dr. K. made sure that the last, small, spot on my leg wouldn't close up; it had to be watched for another fourteen days. But then we couldn't afford to push it any further.

I was not told why I was put in solitary confinement for the eight days following these weeks. Usually only the worst cases went there. The silent, constant and complete solitude is truly a special sort of punishment. After a certain amount of time, you begin to be frightened by your own voice, and yet if you want to avoid collapsing, you must occupy yourself by talking. What sentences would be delivered by a judge if he had sat in solitary confinement for fourteen days, where there wasn't a fly, not a bug, no newspaper, no

161. Correct Polish is *dobry Niemiec*, the "good German."

book, no paper, no pencil, not a nail, no clock and no sun, not a stretch of sky as wide as his hand? There one learns to understand why a notorious criminal never leaves his prison reformed, why, when he is set free, he is even more capable of cleverly and brutally harming society.

Cell fifteen in *oddczia*[162] four is located in the north-east wing of the big H (that is how the penitentiary complex is shaped). I am here with twenty-two others who are called "Foxtrots." They are people who appear to be of Polish descent, but even though they can speak, read and write perfect Polish, they are actually Germans. The rulers hate this category in particular, and these people are especially terrorized at every opportunity. Because of their position in the border zone, they've had to walk the tightrope between alternating German and Polish control since 1914. If asked by the German side about their political views, then they are naturally German; to the other side, as the circumstances changed, they were and are only good Poles.

A high official in the city of T. lost a leg, an arm, and an eye as a German front-line soldier from 1914–1918. Afterwards, fluent in the written and spoken forms of both languages, he continued to work in the municipal administration under Polish rule until 1939. Then the Germans took over the land and obligated him to continue the same position. During this time, he rescued a great succession of Poles from the grip of the German Gestapo. Then the Poles returned in 1945 and sentenced him to twenty years in the penitentiary for collaboration with the Germans.

Another is a farmer, an equally distinguished front-line soldier from 1914–18 and seriously disabled. He spent the interim period between the wars pretty much the same way, and then was sentenced to fifteen years because he beat up a kid who was trying to rob him.

The former judge and then lawyer D. fared similarly. He officiated under the different regimes, and because he had also passed judgment on Poles in his capacity as a judge, he was put behind bars for life.

The priests preached the word of God in Polish as well as

---

162. *Oddział* means department, ward, or branch.

German, which "they never should have done." Because of it, they were stuck here indefinitely. The German authorities transferred a number of men from all parts of Germany to the occupied Polish region as officials or trustees, and because they had the bad luck of missing their last chances to return, they are locked up here without being sentenced.

A group of illiterate Poles who are serving ten to fifteen years for robbery, murder, etc. complete the mosaic in cell fifteen. These are fiends who, because they have enough time, are repeatedly devising new forms of harassment with which they, under the protection of the authorities, deliberately and persistently torment their cellmates. Woe to him who resists. They inform against the victim; he is called out of the cell. The *speziallnie* or one of his assistants trained for this kind of thing tears the man to pieces. Every *zellownie* has to give a report every third day. Frequently a victim is then shoved back into the cell with crushed ribs, knocked-out teeth or something similar. He fell down the staircase. He never dares say that he was beaten.

Christmas day 1947 is no different from the days before or after. Through the walls we can hear an organ playing and the bells for Mass. This massive former cloister was constructed in the fourteenth century. A few of us get on our knees in the shadow of the cross — directly under it; it hangs on the walls in the alcoves of the *oddczias*, where human beings are beaten into cripples during High Mass. At the same time in the next building, the motors drone and the saws squeal, and in a small former chapel, where the walls are still preserved with frescoes of saints, a remaining confessional is used as a toilet. There is plenty of time here to brood over these things.

The religious prisoner has to endure being stripped and chased around the bare cement floor; his tormentors grab at him while making the filthiest jokes, and then he has to wait in front of his plank bed until both the homosexual brats have spent themselves.[163] Intervene? Break it up? Impossible, if you don't want to be torn to pieces, if you want to make it out of here at all, if you want to live.

---

163. Whether sexual abuse is being described here is ambiguous.

From the beginning, the rabble gave some respect to those who were completely indifferent to everything and everyone. It was said that they never knew what to do with me; they couldn't find any reasons to attack me.

There were some jailers who treated me, in contrast to the others, almost politely, and intentionally overlooked things during the frequent raids and searches. On the bi-weekly bathing day, the guys had their fun by running the showers with either boiling hot or ice-cold water. No one was permitted to slip away, but, stubborn as a mule, I nonetheless managed to disappear without being disciplined.

During my time in the infirmary, the lawyer D. requested permission to send a letter in my name to the top Polish military authorities. In a three-page letter written in Polish, he conveyed, among other things, that as a POW my conviction by a civilian court should never have taken place, that I was put here unjustly, that I demand a new trial etc. I signed the letter in the presence of a jailer, but I never figured out whether it was sent and arrived at the correct address. "In any case," my "colleague" said, "It will certainly be read by the administration, and you can only stand to gain from it."

One day I am taken "*na Büro*" again, where again I am charged the old legal costs in the amount of one thousand five hundred *zlotys*.

"Take down a statement, and then I will be able to pay." The typist actually lets me dictate to him and then says only "*Kolera.*"

"I must be permitted," I said, "to write a short letter to my brother in the U.S.A., who is a senator[164] there and for whom it would be a pleasure to send the equivalent in dollars directly to the Polish government in Warsaw." I got the feeling that news of such relations spread through the circles in the administration here.

One day I am told that a *patschka* (package)[165] has arrived for me. Assuming that it was a mistake (who could have sent me a package?), I go to the mail room where I am told to pay five hundred

---

164. This is a complete fabrication; Thiel's brother August, to whom Thiel sent this memoir, was a ship captain. It did not need explanation in the text, since his brother would see the irony and the joke, not to mention the ploy.

165. Correct Polish is *paczka*.

zlotys in customs duties. The parcel is from the U.S.A. My disappointment is immense. Where am I supposed to get even a single *zloty*? Allegedly, the package is returned to the sender. At that time in Poland, you could get fourteen-hundred *zlotys* for one dollar on the black market. A few days later, I am notified of a second package and the same customs duties. The same big disappointment.

On February 5th the usual evening soup has just been served when a jailer appears in the cell door with free-passage papers. He ushers me out with all of my things. A new dirty trick? I quickly go outside, and since he is one of the more reasonable ones, I ask him where I'm going and why. "*Do dom*"[166] (home). "Get your things from the store-room immediately; early tomorrow you will be on a transport crossing the Oder."

It is too wonderful to be true; the information cannot drive away my doubt. My gear had been prepared for me at the store-room. The exchange took place very quickly. The old crumpled uniform made the prisoner into a battered soldier again, and then a cell closed behind me once more — I hoped for the last time.

The next morning, a perfumed, gloved youth in a special uniform takes me to the administration. A brand new machine gun dangles on a shoulder strap. The second in command appears before us, the same one who earlier wanted to prevent committing me and my young comrade to prison. He obviously wanted to deliver me this joy himself; he said only that I was free to go home.

"And why," I asked "this heavily armed escort?"

"That's the regulation!" Then this Polish officer, who always behaves extremely civilly, holds out the cigarette box to me. I am released.

This pomaded[167] soldier responsible for my safety has a problem, for he must transport a prisoner out of prison and not to prison. He therefore will pay less attention, and soon we have a serious conversation about that. His papers call for P[otulitz]., where

166. In Polish, *do domu* means "to go home."
167. Probably referring to a fragrant ointment, not necessarily a hair dressing. See the previous description of the soldier as "perfumed."

in the next few days a transport will be sent off *na Odra*. Do I want to give him my word that I won't run away?

"Yes, I can give you my word."

"Do you have anything against going to P[otulitz]. one day later? I want to take a little detour and visit some friends."

"That's agreeable to me."

"Good, let's eat now." We have this nice conversation in a train compartment, which the young soldier commandeered for himself and his dangerous criminal. Then he places his well-filled briefcase in front of us. Big open-faced sandwiches, sausage, and a small bottle of schnapps appear from inside. My taste-buds are delighted; my stomach will have to worry about digestion. After the meal, and most importantly, come the schnapps and a cigarette.

We walk from some station to a town. We pass an inn only to return and enter it; my guard appears to be known there. His wallet is just as well-stuffed as his breakfast bag. The bottle circulates. In Poland, for sake of simplicity, they drink straight out of the bottle unless they're acting very refined, in which case they use coffee cups. It isn't long before faces are flushed. A great brawl begins while I am sitting in the warm kitchen, getting my pockets filled with bread and sausage by the friendly hostess. Then I grab the groggy guard and his machine gun and stride into the clear, frosty evening.

The guard livens up again in the next town and, looking for a place to stay, drums out his friend (the chief magistrate). His wife makes us a meal and then prepares a thick fur bed for me in their own bedroom. The machine gun dangles on the bedpost, remaining unnoticed by its owner until morning.

After a good breakfast, the altogether pompous, budding warrior leaves to visit more friends with his *Niemniez*. The day and the following night pass in much the same way as the previous day. I am not unhappy; my stomach succeeds in digesting the unusual things. Then, after a short train ride, we end up in old N[akel]., where I had been sentenced. In a final, quiet beer-house, I help to change the dates on the transport papers with a knife and eraser.

I reach camp P[otulitz]. with mixed feelings. Will there perhaps be another quarantine soon? If so, then I hope that the transport will set out in the next couple of days.

The admissions ceremony was hardly changed from my earlier time here. A new personal questionnaire is filled out. At first I protest the designation as a civilian prisoner, but the woman writing persuades me otherwise.

The transport to be arranged is actually supposed to be for civilian prisoners. As a soldier, I wouldn't have any business on it. Therefore, to help me, she "inadvertently" took a different form, which later proved to be the perfectly right thing to do.

My former *kierownik*, who found out about my return through my companions, cut short the usual twenty-one days in quarantine. He came on the third day and took me back to my old workplace. I had two packages from the U.S.A. in P[otulitz]. I was able to persuade a Pole to redeem them for me, and then divided up the contents with him. Despite that, I was extremely happy, especially since there were two beautiful cardigans in one of the packages. They had to be deposited in the store-room, and later, hardly worn, they disappeared from there without a trace.

The seven-month waiting period that followed (or more accurately, the period of heavy labor) once again brought me to a physical low point. Constant nightshifts — because the torment of the bed bugs became unbearable — coupled with the meager rations and the unreasonably high work-requirement, combined with the nerve-racking feeling that the *kierownik* might not name me for the still uncertain transport, have temporarily made even my strong resistance grow weary. The awkward attacks of weakness and dizziness, things I had never known before, increased with violent sweating, as did the swelling all over my body.

One day in May, one of the notorious barracks visits took place again. Those of us on nightshift were awakened and then stood outside in formation in a cold drizzle, clothed in only a shirt and our underclothes. It took about four hours, long enough for the bloodhounds inside to rummage through any and everything completely and indiscriminately. I was never really able to get rid of a cold after that. Presumably, my heart problems[168] are also a result of that day.

---

168. The German here, *Herzknacks*, is a common colloquialism for *Herzfehler*, which can mean "cardiac defects" or "valvular disease of the heart — VDH."

"Unfortunately we cannot help you. Trust in your iron nature, and we'll hope that your lungs are all right." That was the medicine and the medical advice during the following weeks of fever, when my body simply did not want cooperate; it didn't seem to belong to me at all anymore.

Nevertheless, I had to work. Otherwise my rations would be reduced, which was synonymous with death. A reduction in work meant the ruthless cancellation of Kettle I; on the other hand, by fulfilling the quota, one ran the risk of being deleted from any transport list because of his top quality work.

But the time came when for several days a number of people were called who were suitable for the transport. Almost at the end of this operation, I, too, am transferred to the barracks that had been emptied for this purpose. But several more anxious weeks pass by until one night, as usual, the written formalities are taken care of. The next night we finally move off. In groups, we are frisked for the last time in another barracks. First the women, and then we follow.

Once more we experience Polish inhumanity; they say their farewells with the same kind of behavior we've known thus far. We are ruthlessly and brutally slapped, beaten, and kicked, the women just as much as the men; our pathetic bags are torn to pieces, scattered, and ransacked. Our clothes are ripped from our bodies, and they inquire as to whether there is a second shirt, a second pair of pants, jewelry or a piece of paper. Our shoes are turned inside out and examined, and when the victim has finally been searched, he may bundle together his remaining, scattered possessions, walk away with another kick to his body, making room for the next victim.

No one complains. No one sheds any tears for his blanket, his socks, or for that one handkerchief that had been saved so carefully. Many came out of the inspection without any baggage at all. Despite the ill-treatment, the faces are happy. It seems that we're really going home.

No one will ever be able to forget these beasts in human form, in the uniforms with the Polish national emblem. They could have saved themselves trouble and made things easier. They needed only to make the request — no one would have refused to leave the camp naked.

I am pushed into the tumult — already half undressed — with one of the last groups. I take advantage of a peak in the chaos to disappear untouched as one who had already been searched, and whose stuff had just been taken. Outside the P[otulitz]. barbed-wire stands a row of trucks, which are supposed to take the infants, the old men and women who are unable to march, and their bags. Those of us marching, under surveillance by guards on bikes, thought that was a very noble deed. But the thieves still managed a final raid — the few bundles and boxes that were supposed to be put on one truck were thoughtfully looked after and loaded onto different trucks. And those who were transported, then waited in the N[akel]. train station — in vain — for the arrival of all that was left of their possessions.

The transport, with about eleven-hundred people, rolls westward under Polish-Russian command. No one can really understand how this works; one controls the other.[169] The Oder now is three days behind us. Since that point we haven't seen any of the despised, four-cornered Polish caps. The Russians hardly draw attention to themselves. Sad, the sight of once fertile tracts of land, the devastated, burnt-out cities and towns, the ruins that once were train stations, the main routes reduced to single-track lines. A generation of work will not be enough to blot out these marks of destruction.

Apparently our destination is the well-known city of E[rfurt]. in Thuringia. The transport is split up here and taken to two quarantine camps. I get to W[eimar?]. and intend to make it through the twelve days that are stipulated for quarantine, first of all so that I can acquire official papers, and also to size up the surrounding area. I have been determined to escape ever since we crossed the Oder. Clearly up to that point, an escapee hardly had any chance of making it. Here, however, it must be possible and had to be attempted.

As a "specialist," I am transferred from here to a state-run experimental farm in the region of G[otha]., and in addition to a

---

169. During this period it was often difficult to determine whether the Russians or the Poles were in charge in a certain area. The Poles were setting up administrations in places, but often their orders overlapped with those of the Russian administrations, even until the mid fifties.

medical quarantine certificate, I'm given a travel document for me
and a group of others who are being housed in the same region. The
Russian-led camp administration even gives me one hundred East
German marks with it.

Then I make myself scarce and spend several days checking out
the surveillance along the border. I finally decided that I didn't want
to run the risk of being caught and shipped off to Siberia. Not far
from the border at the small train station of V[acha].,[170] a train runs
at intervals of a few hours shuttling railroad workers. It draws me
like a magnet, especially since in the open country, the Russian
guards sat in the tree tops and searched the region with binoculars.
The surveillance of the train station was also in the hands of Ivan
and the East German railroad police.

I ask one of the officers for a light, at the same time inquiring
whether he had been a soldier.

"Yes, long enough, already half-forgotten." I give him a brief
account of my situation, and ask him if he could give me a tip. He
did. I must move carefully and under full cover. In twenty-five minutes an engine will stop at that spot there, and I have to jump onto
it as quickly as possible. The engineer will understand.

As a precaution, he immediately strikes up a conversation with
the Ivan on duty and draws him away. And then the locomotive
pokes up, very slowly. As quickly as possible I climb the ladder and
get under full cover. After a few minutes, the engine stops again.
The engineer and stoker don't want to take my last cigarettes. This
time I calmly climb down the embankment to the street that leads to
the town of Ph[ilippsthal].[171] in the American zone. I've made it.

On the street towards the train station, I haven't gone a hundred meters when a strange looking vehicle brakes sharply beside
me. Three very well-kept, good-looking blond figures in well-fitting
uniforms jump out of the crate[172] and quickly agree to speak in German.

"Papers?"

170. In Thuringia, then East Germany.
171. In Hesse, then West Germany.
172. Jalopy, box, as a jeep would look.

"None."

"Where are you coming from?"

I responded briefly.

"Where are you going?"

I told them that just as quickly.

Then a quick military salute.

The jeep buzzes away with its friendly passengers and their white-striped helmets. I have met American soldiers. Then I stretch out along the embankment and let my nerves die down.

Editor's Epilogue

Upon his return to Germany, Thiel discovered that his wife had left him for another man, perhaps having believed that he was dead or would not return. He later remarried and lived in Kassel, working as a siding salesman. His business never prospered, however, and he and his new wife sometimes still received support from his brother in America.

The war left scars on everyone in Germany and everyone in Thiel's family, and Thiel, in particular, despite his impressive strength, never

Hans Thiel with his second wife, Ruth.

Left: Thiel, Ruth, and Thiel's brother in America, August Thiel, to whom Hans sent the memoir. Photograph taken in 1963. *Right*: Hans Thiel, many years after the war.

completely overcame the physical and emotional wounds caused by the wolves of war. He died on June 13, 1974, at the age of 72.

Appendix A: A Note on Agrarian Policy and Farm Life Under the Third Reich

As a long-time farmer, Hans Thiel naturally refers to agricultural subjects and governmental farm policies when he describes his life prior to his conscription, and he does so, understandably, with little explanatory comment. The following should give the reader a context to understand this first part of his memoir, which deals with the rural homefront under the Third Reich.

In 1933, the Nazi government instituted an agricultural program called the *Reichsnährstand*, led by Walter Darré.[173] It was an attempt to aid the German farmer, especially the small farmers, by reorganizing agrarian marketing, regulating production, and fixing prices on his goods. The literal translation of the German *Reichsnährstand*, "Reich Food Estate," does not reveal all of the Nazi aims for this program. The *Reichsnährstand* was part of a larger process by which they looked to glorify the land and the soil, an attempt epitomized in the phrase "*Blut und Boden*" ("Blood and Soil"). While appealing to the people's connection with the land and their aversion to industrial, urban life, this phrase also played on a feeling of "blood ties" with fellow Germans. In doing so, however, the words also incited the distrust of and even animosity towards foreigners and those not considered "blood Germans," including, especially, the Jewish population.

Essentially, the *Reichsnährstand* was an effort to exalt the farmer and to integrate him into the state's more general political plans, and Thiel concedes that although farmers under the Third Reich prospered unlike ever before,

---

173. Darré was the *Reichsminister für Ernährung und Landwirtschaft* (Reich Minister of Food and Agriculture) and the *Reichsbauernführer* (Reich Farmers' Leader). He was considered one of the primary Nazi ideologists, and although Hitler eventually removed him from his posts for disagreements during the war, he was sentenced to five years at the Military Tribunals in Nuremberg.

the Party's ulterior motive was only to garner support for the regime. Eventually, when the Nazis' position as ruling body grew more secure, the *Reichsnährstand* became another means by which they could regulate industry to suit their goals. All food producers were required to take part in the organization and refusal was considered a direct attack on the state. Darré and his staff, therefore, completely controlled all of the farmers, and farmers like Thiel, who disagreed with other aspects of Nazi ideology, were in danger of losing the benefit of the policies designed to help those in agriculture.

Thiel also mentions the Law of Hereditary Entitlement (*Erbhofgesetz*), another important set of laws designed to help the farmer, and which well complemented the *Reichsnährstand*. An *Erbhofbauer* was a *Bauer* (a farmer or peasant) whose farm met the requirements of an *Erbhof*, literally translated as "inheritance land." As Thiel explains, the farm was supposed to meet certain size requirements, and fifty-five percent of the farmed land met these requirements.[174] It could not be subdivided, mortgaged, or sold, and was supposed to pass to the farmer's eldest son. Thus, the farmer would enjoy fixed prices, and he was assured that his land would remain in his family. Yet despite the many rights and honors enjoyed by the *Erbhofbauer*, Darré revealed the true intentions of the program when he pronounced at Weimar in February 1935, "It must be made clear to the peasant that we have not created special laws for him for the sake of his bonny blue eyes [*schöne Augen*] but because he has a job to do for Germany."[175] As with much in Nazi policy, Thiel shows that what first seemed to be a positive program was undercut from the beginning, for it was always designed to cater to Party interests.

Nevertheless, most Germans agreed with these and some of the Nazis' other early policies, many of which enjoyed wide support for good reason. For example, Thiel recognized the programs of the *Hitler Jugend*[176] to be paramilitary programs promoting the ideals and aims of the Party; nonetheless, he believed in the importance of teaching young people how to exercise and how to work. The labor service program, which became compulsory on June 26, 1935, arranged for all youths, regardless of sex or wealth, to work for six months on a farm, at a construction site, or in a similar labor activity. As a result, class barriers were crossed, and everyone had an experience that Thiel believed would be helpful later in life. It was a good idea. Yet as always with the Nazis, the labor service program was a good idea that quickly became corrupted. The program proved to be the perfect opportunity to drill the youths in propaganda and prepare them for their military service, an opportunity that the Nazis exploited, and which Thiel found repugnant.

174. J.E. Farquharson. *The Plough and the Swastika: The NSDAP and Agriculture in Germany 1928–45*. London and Beverly Hills: SAGE Publications, 1976 (p.63).
175. Farquharson, (p. 57).
176. Hitler Youth — the obligatory youth programs under the Nazis.

Appendix B:
Thiel's Sojourn

A reader will quickly discover that the journey recounted in Thiel's memoir — a narrative covering more than three years of combat and imprisonment — is difficult to track on a map. Habitually casual in identifying locations, Thiel clearly had no intention of constructing a graphic chart of the tangled route he traveled. But unless the reader can follow Thiel's movements, he will not grasp the physical hardship that the long journey inflicted upon Thiel, and as a result, the greater ordeal that he suffered will not be fully appreciated.

Determining Thiel's locations and tracing his movements are difficult tasks for several reasons. First, with few exceptions, Thiel uses only an initial letter to identify locations and people. He gives no explanation for this practice. Perhaps he assumes the reader (his brother, his family) is sufficiently well acquainted with the area that the places need no further identification. Perhaps, for reasons he believes prudent, he wants to avoid identifying someone or something. Or perhaps such a practice is merely a shorthand system for his own reference. In any case, a reader will not recognize many of the cities and towns by the single letters Thiel provides — at least not without considerable research.

Thiel's handling of time presents another problem. His irregular use of tenses, sometimes even within a sentence, has the unintended effect of conflating the present with the past, a confusion which hinders tracing his movements. In addition, Thiel's occasional habit of silently telescoping time complicates the issue even further. For example, in describing his ordeal of moving from one prison camp to another, Thiel might not tell how much time passed in traveling, so a reader will not know whether the distance covered is ten kilometers or a hundred kilometers, making the destination Thiel represents by a single letter even more difficult to identify. Similarly, if, after describing an event at one location, Thiel swiftly shifts (without indicating any passage of time) to describing another incident at a different location, a reader will be at a loss to judge the distance between the two locations. An additional idiosyncrasy is that Thiel often uses the adjective *bekannt* ("well-known," or "familiar") to describe a location. Sometimes he uses this word to say that the place is well known to him, but sometimes he writes as if the reader is in fact acquainted with a place. If a particular reader in the 1940s was, the general reader today certainly is not.

There is another problem, one not of Thiel's making. Identifying locations in his narrative is made especially difficult because of the history, particularly the twentieth-century political history, of the regions in which Thiel travels. The area ranges from as far east as Russia to as far west as central Germany. After World War I, the realignment of the Polish–German borders shifted certain ethnic areas from one national authority to the other. Then, because of Germany's invasion of Poland in 1939 (and its subsequent expulsion in 1945), traditionally ethnic–German regions underwent additional shifts between Polish and German governmental authorities. Accordingly, the names of cities and towns in the area alternated between Polish and German forms.

As a result of these name changes, locating the places mentioned by Thiel on maps and gazetteers is frequently a challenge. Locations that he cites with a single letter — understandably associated with the German name — will often be found in sources and maps of the last fifty years only in their Polish form. Thiel's supplied initial letters, then, are frequently of only limited use for identification purposes. One may, for example, have little trouble recognizing Thiel's reference to the northern coastal town of "F." as today's Frombork in Poland, even though Thiel is referring to the town by its German name, Frauenburg. But Thiel's "S." does not readily identify today's Polish Pila, known to the author as Schneidemühl, and his "N." does not obviously refer to today's Wejherowo in northern Poland, which Thiel knew as Neustadt. A variety of maps dating from World War II — of German origin in particular — consulted in the Library of Congress has been particularly helpful in seeking the identity of the places mentioned by Thiel.

All these problems aside, most of Thiel's sojourn can be traced, and as its tracking unfolds, one comes to have considerable respect for Thiel's detailed accuracy of place despite his reluctance to identify locations explicitly. As it turns out, his offhand remarks often contain the best clues for mapping his long and complicated route. For example, Thiel not only mentions that the city of "K." (where he was incarcerated in a civilian prison) is located north of Bromberg (Bydgoszcz in Polish) at the end of a "narrow-gauge railway," but he also describes various details of its fourteenth-century massive church near the prison. Both features serve to identify "K." as the city Thiel knew as Konitz, known in today's Poland as Chojnice.

Similarly, Thiel places the prison camp at "L." ten kilometers east of Bromberg; shortly afterwards he comments on the scenic view from "L." as

he gazes upon the beauty of the Vistula River valley below. These details identify "L." as the village Thiel knew as Langenau, but which now bears the Polish name Legnowo. With such fragmentary information, many places can be
identified, some with greater certainty than others. Others, of course, continue to resist identification altogether.

As an aid for following Thiel's narrative, a synopsis of the author's movements is provided below (arranged in four parts, in keeping with the edito-
rially organized translation). This synopsis gives a skeletal itinerary of Thiel's
journey from his pre-conscription days in East Prussia to his escape into the
American zone of West Germany years later. Places are identified according
to four degrees of certainty as follows:

1. **Name** Names of places that can be identified with certainty, even when
   they appear in Thiel's text with only an initial letter, are presented in the
   synopsis without any mark.
2. **Name with an asterisk** (*) Names of places that are identified with less
   certainty are marked with an asterisk.
3. **Letter alone** Places that resist identification are left as Thiel presents them
   with an initial letter only.
4. **Name with a query mark** (?) Unidentified places presented with the initial letter alone are, when possible, accompanied by one or more plausible
   conjectures enclosed within parentheses and marked with a question mark.

Locations are cited by the German placenames used by Thiel and, when
the locations are in today's Poland, they are followed by their Polish placenames in square brackets, as in: Danzig [Gdansk]. Any distance cited in kilometers is taken from Thiel's text and has been used to verify the identified
location. The distances Thiel provides are remarkably accurate.

A map by the Office of Strategic Services (1944), a map of wartime Poland
prepared by the United States Army Map Service for the Army Chief of Staff
(1943), and a map of the administrative divisions of post-war Germany prepared for the Department of State (1947) can be found on p. 24, pp. 42, 43,
93, and p. 107, respectively. All maps are reproduced from originals in the Map
and Geographical Division of the Library of Congress, Washington, D.C. Cities
and towns, along with other geographical locations identified in Thiel's memoir, are marked on these maps, allowing the reader to chart Thiel's sojourn.

Part I

In the summer of 1944, Thiel departs from O. (Osterode? [Ostroda?],
though perhaps, but less likely, Ortelsburg? [Szczytno?]) to travel east to build

fortifications as part of a group of men drafted under the *Volksaufgebot* (The People's Levy).

Part II

During his time working with that conscripted contingent, Thiel mentions being at the small fortress of O. (Some cities in eastern Germany were designated by the German government as *Festungen* [fortresses], or stronghold cities, places where German forces were ordered to fight to the last man. Whether O. is such a city or whether it is simply a city or town with an old fortress descriptively cited by Thiel cannot be determined.)

Thiel finally arrives at a Russian-Polish border town, D. after a nearly three-day march from O. What he means by "Russian-Polish border" is impossible to determine. Following the Soviet Union's annexation of the eastern part of Poland in early World War II, the political boundaries of those two countries shifted regularly. Doubtless, however, the site of D. is reasonably far east of Thiel's home district. With the rest of his group, he returns home in autumn to work in the harvest of 1944.

Thiel mentions a training center for anti-tank weaponry in the town of Mielau* [Mława*], south of his farm, as being active in November, 1944, a little over a month after the *Volkssturm* was created.

In January, 1945, Thiel is drafted into the *Volkssturm* and is transported to the town of Kaltenborn* [Zimnawoda*] in *Masuren* [*Mazury*] (also known as *Masurenland* in German), a lake and wooded area southeast of the Gulf of Danzig [*Gdansk*]. Allenstein [Olsztyn], where the Thiel family had a resort home, is the region's most important city in that region, and Passenheim [Pasym], the location of the Thiel farm, is nearby. After spending time at Kaltenborn* [Zimnawoda*], his unit is transported "eighty kilometers" to Guttstadt* [Dobre Miasto*], during which journey he travels by or through Ortelsburg [Szczytno], described as an administrative district town "twenty-two kilometers" from his home near Passenheim [Pasym].

Thiel writes of seeing refugees trying to reach the Vistula [Wisla] River, which would describe a westward flight from the Soviet army. He arrives at Guttstadt* [Dobre Miasto*] mentioning the *Heilsberger Dreieck* (Heilsberger Triangle), a widely dispersed fortified region in East Prussia dating from after World War I. He refers to a small city of R. in the *Heilsberger Dreieck*. With the Soviet army driving from the east and up from the south towards the northern coast, Thiel's unit retreats north to Braunsberg [Braniewo] near the coast of the *Frisches Haff*, which Thiel invariably refers to as the *Haff*—a shallow inlet separated from the Gulf of Danzig [Gdansk] by a long, sand spit.

He proceeds farther north and then west through the coastal towns of Frauenburg [Frombork] and Tolkemit [Tolkmicko] and then to the Vistula [Wisla] River city of Elbing [Elblag], Later, he crosses the *Frisches Haff*, apparently on its frozen surface, arriving at Kahlburg [Krynica Morska], after which he moves west towards Danzig [Gdansk] along the sandy spit separating the *Haff* from the Gulf of Danzig [Gdansk].

On his way to Danzig [Gdansk], Thiel's unit finds lodging at Stutthof [Sztutowo], which was a Nazi concentration camp only a short time earlier, before continuing west to and through Danzig [Gdansk]. He passes Gotenhafen [Gydnia] as he is relocated to Neustadt* [Wejherowo*] west of Gotenhafen [Gydnia] to stand against the Russians who are by then driving towards Danzig [Gdansk] from the west as well as the east and south, having surrounded the city on all sides except from the sea.

Thiel's unit retreats back towards Danzig [Gdansk] and is overrun by Soviet tanks while in sandy trenches, which indicates that he was then near the coast. The date he is overrun is, as he pointedly notes, March 28, 1945, the day Gotenhafen [Gydnia] falls to the Soviet Army. Two days later, Danzig [Gdansk] was captured.

Part III

Thiel is led by his Russian captors on a circuitous western trek through Pomerania [Pomorskie], passing through the cities of Lauenburg [Lebork] and Bütow [Bytow] and various other parts of the region until he is later hospitalized in L. (again Lauenburg? [Lebork?]). The Soviets release him at the time of the armistice a couple of months later and give him papers to proceed to S. (Schneidemühl? [Pila?]).

Part IV

At the railroad station in Bromberg [Bydgoszcz] east of Schneidemühl [Pila], however, Thiel finds himself taken prisoner anew, this time by the Polish authorities, and he is held at Kaltwasser [Zimna], a former Nazi concentration camp just outside of Bromberg [Bydgoszcz]. Some time later, he is transferred to another former Nazi concentration camp overlooking the Vistula (Wisla) River near Langenau [Legnowo], a short distance southeast of Bromberg [Bydgoszcz]. In time, he is moved to Potulitz [Potulice] "twenty kilometers" west of Bromberg [Bydgoszcz] and "eight kilometers" from Nakel [Nakło] to the west. Later he is marched those eight kilometers to Nakel [Nakło] to stand trial, returning to Potulitz [Potulice] after conviction.

Months pass before he goes to S. (Slesin [also Slesin in Polish]), northeast of Potulitz [Potulice] to board a train to Bromberg [Bydgoszcz], anticipating that he will then go west to the Oder [Odra] River. But instead, he is placed on a train traveling north on a "narrow gauge railway" to the civilian prison at Konitz [Chojnice]. After months at Konitz [Chojnice], he is told he will be transported west across the Oder [Odra] River, only to be transported instead south to Nakel [Nakło], turning east yet again to arrive in Bromberg [Bydgoszcz], after which he is reimprisoned at Potulitz [Potulice].

At least seven months later, Thiel is again transported to Nakel [Nakło] and then finally farther west to East Germany with Erfurt in Thuringia the destination, and then on to nearby Weimar for quarantine. He has finally crossed the Oder [Odra] River into Germany but he is not yet at liberty since he is in the Soviet zone of that divided post-war country. He is placed on a farm in the region of Gotha (a rural district with its main city of the same name) for processing, where he is given papers along with East German marks. He makes his way to the train station of Vacha, a small East German town near the border of the American zone of West Germany, where he hops a train when it halts briefly, later to climb off and "calmly" walk across the border separating Thuringia (East Germany) and Hesse (West Germany). He has arrived at the small village of Philippsthal in the American zone.

Appendix C: Placenames

All places listed below are cities, towns, and other geographical locations mentioned or referred to in Thiel's memoir, usually only by the initial letter of the German name. Placenames in areas where German–Polish border changes have occurred are listed by both national names, the languages of which are identified by either G (German) or P (Polish). Additional descriptive details are provided in some cases and are always attached to the German or English forms.

Allenstein (G), Olsztyn (P)

Braunsberg (G), Braniewo (P)

Braniewo (P), Braunsberg (G)

Bromberg (G), Bydgoszcz (P): a subcamp of the Stutthof concentration camp complex.

Bütow (G), Bytow (P)

Bydgoszcz (P), see Bromberg (G)

Bytow (P) Bütow (G)

Chojnice (P), Konitz (G)

Danzig (G), Gdansk (P)

East Prussia: an ethnic German area that was separated from contiguous Germany after World War I by a strip of land known as the Polish Corridor.

Elbing (G), Elblag (P): an East Prussian city near the *Frisches Haff*.

Elblag (P), see Elbing (G)

Erfurt: in the southeastern part of East Germany, the capital of Thuringia.

Frauenburg (G), Frombork (P)

Frisches Haff (G), Zalew Wiślany (P): an inlet of the Gulf of Gdansk (Danzig) separated from the Gulf by a narrow sand spit. Known also as the Vistula Lagoon.

Frombork (P), Frauenburg (G)

Gdansk (P), Danzig (G)

Gotha: a city in Thuringia in a district of the same name. West of Erfurt.

Gotenhafen (G) Gdynia (P)

Guttstadt (G), Dobre Milasto (P)

Gdynia (P), Gotenhafen (G)

Haff: a colloquial form of *Frisches Haff*.

Heilsberger Dreieck: a wide-spread series of fortifications in East Prussia.

Hesse (English), Hessen (G): A region in west-central Germany (in former West Germany).

Kahlberg (G), Krynica Morska (P)

Kaltenborn (G), Zimnawoda (P)

Kaltwasser (G), Zimna or Zimna Woda (P): a Polish work camp where Thiel was incarcerated (near Bromberg).

Kassel: a city in the northernmost part of the American sector of West Germany where Thiel spent his last years.

Königsberg (G): formerly the capital of East Prussia, but after 1945 a part of the Soviet Union (Russia) and known as Kaliningrad.

Konitz (G), Chojnice (P)

Krynica Morska (P), Kahlberg (G)

Langenau (G), Legnowo (P)

Lauenburg (G), Lebork (P): a subcamp of the Stutthof concentration camp.

Lebork (P), see Lauenburg (G)

Legnowo (P), Langenau (G)

Masuren (G), Mazury (P): an area in northeast Poland and East Prussia.

Mazury (P), see Masuren (G)

Mielau (G), Mława (P)

Mława (P), Mielau (G)

Nakel (G), Nakło (P)

Nakło (P), Nakel (G)

Neustadt (G), Wejherowo (P)

Oder (G), Odra (P): a major river forming part of the border between post-war East Germany and Poland.

Oder-Neisse line: the post-war border of East Germany and Poland running from the Baltic Sea to Czechoslovakia formed by the Oder and Neisse rivers.

Odra (P), see Oder (G)

Olsztyn (P), Allenstein (G)

Ortelsburg (G), Szccytn (P)

Osterode (G), Ostroda (P)

Ostroda (P), Osterode (G)

Philippsthal: in the American sector of Germany near the border of the Russian sector.

Pila (P), Schneidemühl (G)

Pomerania (English), Pommern (G), Pomorskie (P): the Baltic coastal area west of Danzig (Gdansk) of what is now northeastern Poland, part of Germany prior to 1945.

Pommern (G), see Pomerania

Pomorskie (P), see Pomerania

Potsdam: in East Germany.

Potulitz (G), Potulice (P): a labor camp, part of the Stutthof concentration camp complex.

Potulice (P), see Potulitz (G)

Riga: the capital city of Latvia.

Schneidemühl (G), Pila (P)

Stutthof (G), Sztutowo (P): a major concentration camp complex south of Danzig.

Slesin (G and P)

Szccytn (P), Ortelsburg (G)

Sztutowo (P), see Stutthof (G)

Thuringia (English), Thüringen (G): region of central Germany (in former East Germany).

Tolkemit (G), Tolkmicko (P)

Tolkmicko (P), Tolkemit (G)

Vacha: in East Germany on the border with the American sector of West Germany.

Vistula (English), Weichsel (G) Wisla (P): the principal river of Poland, emptying into the Baltic Sea near Danzig.

Weichsel (G), see Vistula

Weimar: city in Thuringia.

Wejherowo (P), Neustadt (G)

Wisla (P), see Vistula

Zalew Wiślany (P), see Frisches Haff (G)

Zimna or Zimna Woda (P), see Kaltwasser (G)

Zimnawoda (P), Kaltenborn (G)

Glossary

Terms defined in Thiel's text or in explanatory footnotes are not listed below unless they appear elsewhere in the memoir without identification or definition.

Capo: a prisoner who served as a supervisor of the labor force in camps.

Chef: a boss, or head.

Dawai (Thiel's spelling), *davai* (correct Russian): "forward" or "fast," as a command.

Erbhofbauer: a farmer whose property met the requirements of the *Erbhofgesetz*, the Law of Hereditary Entitlement. See Appendix A on agriculture and farming for a discussion of related terms.

Gauleiter: the leader of the largest administrative region of the Nazi Party (Gau), appointed by Hitler.

Gauleitung: a directorate of Nazi Party members in a Gau.

Gestapo: the Nazi secret police.

Hilfswillige: Auxiliary (non–German) volunteers. They were primarily Soviets who worked as laborers in non-combat roles for the German military. At times, however, they were used in combat roles.

Hiwis: slang for *Hilfswillige*.

Ivan: the term used by the Germans for Russians.

Kettle I: a desirable portion of food served to prisoners, distributed on the basis of their labor.

Kettle II: an insufficient portion of food served to prisoners, distributed on the basis of their labor. The weakest, therefore, would likely receive inadequate nourishment.

Kierownik (pl. **kierownicy**): slang for the person in a work camp responsible for productivity and discipline within a particular occupational branch of labor.

Kolera Niemniez (Thiel's spelling), *cholera niemiec* (correct Polish): Damned German.

Kurvie sinn (Thiel's spelling), *skurwysyn* (correct Polish): Son of a bitch.

L. Schein: an abbreviated form of *landwirtschaftlicher Schein*, food-stamp-like allotments distributed during the war (literally, agricultural banknote).

LKW: the abbreviation for *Lastkraftwagen*, a shipping truck.

LMG: the abbreviation for *Leichtes Maschinengewehr*, light machine gun.

majontek (Thiel's spelling), *majątek* (correct Polish): farm.

mangel-wurzel: a root vegetable used for forage.

Mauser: a widely used make of firearm.

na Büro: "to the office" (the first word is Polish, the second German).

Niemniez (Thiel's spelling), *nemets* (correct Russian), *niemiec* (correct Polish): a German.

NSDAP: the abbreviation for the *Nationalsozialistische Deutsche Arbeiterpartei*, the National Socialist German Worker's Party, or the Nazi Party.

oddczia (Thiel's spelling), *oddział* (correct Polish): department, ward, or branch.

oggien (Thiel's spelling), *ogień* (correct Polish): slang for a light for a cigarette. It actually means "fire."

Pan: the Polish word that translates roughly as "Mr." or "Gentleman." Often, as in German, the term prefaces other titles, as in "Herr Doktor."

Panzerfaust (pl. **Panzerfäuste**): a single-use anti-tank weapon similar to the American bazooka.

PKW: the abbreviation for *Personenkraftwagen*, a private motorcar.

Reichsnährstand: See Appendix A, "A Note on Agrarian Policy and Farming Under the Third Reich."

SA: *Sturmabteilung*, commonly known as Storm Troopers, a paramilitary unit of the Nazi Party

Sandhill: The term (*Sandberg*) that the prisoners commonly used for the place where the camp dead were taken for disposal.

SMG: abbreviation for *Schweres Maschinengewehr*, a heavy machine gun.

Speziallnie (Thiel's spelling), *specjalny* (correct Polish): "special" as in "special branch," an abbreviated reference to the Polish secret police.

SS: *Schutzstaffel* or "defense squad." Directed by Heinrich Himmler, the SS was the elite police force of the Nazi Party. It was originally Adolf Hitler's personal guard, but it became a potent military and political force. The SS operated the concentration camps.

Volkssturm: See the editor's introduction for a discussion of this civilian-military body.

Wehrmacht: the regular German army.

Zellownie (Thiel's spelling), *celowny* (correct Polish): cell leader.

Zloty (Thiel's spelling), *złoty* (pl. *złotych*) (correct Polish): the Polish monetary unit.

Index

Most names of locations are provided in their German forms; see Placenames (Appendix C) for cross references to Polish names.